# TASSEL MAKING
# FOR BEGINNERS

# TASSEL MAKING
# FOR BEGINNERS

Enid Taylor

GUILD OF MASTER CRAFTSMAN PUBLICATIONS LTD

First published 1997 by
Guild of Master Craftsman Publications Ltd,
166 High Street, Lewes,
East Sussex BN7 1XU

Reprinted 1998 (twice), 1999

ISBN 1 86108 062 X

Photography by Gavin Mist
Line drawings by John Yates

Designed by Lovelock & Co
Typeface: Sabon
Colour separation in Singapore under the supervision of
MRM Graphics, Winslow, Buckinghamshire, UK
Printed in Hong Kong by H & Y Printing Ltd

*To my husband Terry, without whose patience and encouragement this book would not have been written*

# Acknowledgements

I would like to record my thanks to Liz Inman for her help and encouragement in getting me started on this book, and to Bryony Bénier for her detailed advice. My thanks also to Gavin Mist for his patience, kindness and skill in producing the photographs.

# Measurements

Although care has been taken to ensure that imperial measurements are true and accurate, they are only conversions from metric. Throughout the book instances may be found where a metric measurement has slightly varying imperial equivalents, because in each particular case the closest imperial equivalent has been given. Care should be taken to use either imperial or metric measurements consistently.

# CONTENTS

# CHAPTER I

# INTRODUCING
# TASSELS

T assels are fun. They come in all sorts of sizes, colours and materials. Their function is often purely decorative, but tassels do have practical uses as well. Attaching a tassel can make small objects such as keys easier to find, and they can be made into light pulls and bell pulls as well as the more usual curtain tie-backs (see Fig 1.1). They have been used for centuries as part of traditional costumes and have been adapted both by dress designers to adorn their clothes and by interior designers to enhance upholstery and soft furnishings.

Fig 1.1 A selection of tassels for different purposes.

A tassel can be formally defined as 'an ornamental hanging tuft of thread', but tassels today are often rather more than that. We have available to us a huge variety of threads and other materials which can add to the decorative qualities of every tassel.

Tassels are easy to make. Once you have grasped the three basic methods, there are unlimited possibilities for producing exciting effects by using different threads, decorative finishes and endlessly varied combinations. The size, shape, colour, thread type and decoration of the tassel must be appropriate to its intended use, and advice on all these points is given throughout the book as each method is explained.

The first method, which I call the 'one-part' method, is quick and easy. It produces a tassel made of thread only (see Fig 1.2), which can be embellished in a variety of ways. Chapter 4 explains the basic method and if you have never made a tassel before, you should read this chapter and try a practice tassel before going further into the book (Chapter 3, on making cords, is also essential reading to begin with). Chapter 5 shows seven different ways of decorating one-part tassels.

Fig 1.2 Basic
one-part thread
tassels.

The second method uses a solid shape (usually wooden) which is covered to make an attractive head to the tassel (see Fig 1.3). The skirt of the tassel is made separately and then attached to the base of

Fig 1.3 Two-
part tassels with
covered wooden
heads.

the head. I call this the 'two-part' method. Very elaborate tassels can be made in this way. The head and the skirt can have different types of thread and because they are made separately more decoration can be applied. The basic two-part method is set out in Chapter 6. Chapter 7 offers five very varied ways to decorate two-part tassels with covered heads.

The third method is a variation on the two-part method mentioned above and involves a polished head (rather than one covered in thread) with the skirt of the tassel fixed either round a neck groove or inside the central hole (see Fig 1.4). Fixing the skirt inside the polished head is especially useful if the tassel is to be handled frequently so, for example, this would be the best method to use for a light pull. Chapter 8 gives instructions for making polished-head tassels.

This book deals with the basic methods as an introduction to tassel making, and offers a number of different decorative ideas for each type of tassel to demonstrate the range of possibilities. This is only a fraction of what can be achieved, however, and once you are familiar with the principles you will be able to start experimenting with different effects and designing your own tassels.

Fig 1.4 Two-part, polished-head tassels, some with the skirts fixed inside.

# CHAPTER 2

# MATERIALS AND EQUIPMENT

You do not need large amounts of expensive equipment to make a tassel. The thread will probably be the most costly part, depending on the types and makes you decide to use. The advice on different threads included here is not exhaustive by any means, but it will show you the wide range of possibilities available today. The best thing is to go and look at the threads themselves and decide what you like best. For the rest of the basic equipment you need, you will probably find that you have most of it at home already.

## Threads

It is possible to make tassels from any material that will hang or drape. I have successfully made tassels incorporating feathers, beads, string and leather strands, but the usual basic material is thread. Some threads are easier to use than others because they hang well and do not fray when cut. There is a vast choice of type and colour, including natural fibres such as cotton, linen, silk and wool, man-made fibres such as rayon, and metallic threads. Many of the threads I use are from the range offered by Madeira Threads (UK) Ltd, which are widely available. DMC and Anchor offer comparable products (see Fig 2.1), and advice on various types of thread is given overleaf.

Fig 2.1  A selection of threads: Sticku, Rayon 40, Decor, Ombre, Burmilana, Renaissance wool and Cotton Perle.

**TIP**  In the past I have used some very interesting unnamed or unbranded threads and cords, only to find that they are unavailable at a later date. If you are contemplating buying non-standard threads, my advice is to buy more than you might need in the first place to allow for mistakes or repeat tassels.

## Natural fibres
### Cotton
Cotton thread has the minimum swing that a tassel needs to give it the correct, luxurious look, but it is still useful and inexpensive. My first tassel was made from six-strand embroidery cotton decorated with a heavy metallic, ready-made cord and was very easy to work. Cotton Perle is the best cotton thread for tassels because it can be used as a cord for binding or hanging as well as for making the tassel itself.

### Linen
Linen certainly has some ability to swing, but is not high on my list of preferred threads. It is expensive and not that easy to find. There are some hand-dyed linen threads sold for embroidery, but as these are usually cut into lengths suitable for the embroiderer, they are uneconomical for the tassel maker.

### Silk
Silk threads are always a joy to use, however you decide to incorporate them into your tassel. Depending on its manufacture, silk can add either a shiny or a matt quality to your work. It is usually expensive and I would therefore only include it in a really special project and then only after practising on less costly threads. There are many beautiful hand-dyed silks available, but bear in mind that these are produced in cut lengths like the linen threads; you need to order them specially if you want the thread in continuous hanks.

**TIP** It will be necessary to have to hand some 'tying thread' which can be used temporarily to hold the tassel before the decorative finish is applied. I usually use Cotton Perle 12, Cebelia, or redundant lengths of a six-strand embroidery thread.

### Wool
For me, wool comes top of the natural fibres for tassel making. It has swing and bulk and is available in a wide variety of colours, thicknesses and qualities. You can make an excellent, inexpensive tassel from the wool left after knitting or tapestry work.

Appleton's or Renaissance crewel wools and Paterna tapestry wool are all extremely useful when making tassels for trimming soft furnishings. Appleton's have a large colour range, while the Renaissance wools are all in lovely soft colours.

Make sure you buy crewel wool in hanks, not the short lengths often sold for embroidery use. Appleton's crewel wool, for example, is sold in 25g (1oz) hanks which consist of 62m (68yd) of thread.

Paterna wool can be stranded after the tassel is made (see the wool tassel project on pages 81–6), which increases the bulk to give a more luxurious result.

The wools can be mixed in texture and thickness, or other fibres can be added to give a more sumptuous effect without great expense – for example, by adding a small amount of shiny silk to the outer layers of a mainly wool tassel skirt you will completely change the look of the tassel.

## Man-made fibres

Man-made fibres are very popular with tassel makers because many of them have great swingability. They are manufactured in a huge variety of colours, thicknesses and textures and so can be used to make tassels for all sorts of purposes. The following comments are on threads from the range offered by Madeira Threads, because these are the ones that I use, but similar products are available from other manufacturers and your local needlework or haberdashery shop will be able to advise you.

### Rayon 30

This is my particular favourite: a strong machine embroidery thread sold on small reels holding 150m (164yd), which is enough to make a substantial key tassel. The same thread is also called Sticku and sold on cops holding 625m (683yd). It is, of course, more economical to buy the larger amount, but not so easy to tell how much you have used if you wish to make a number of tassels from one cop. For more information on quantities of thread needed, see the individual projects in later chapters. There are 30 plain colours and 6 variegated colours available as Rayon 30 on the smaller reels, and 174 plain colours available as Sticku on the 625m (683yd) cops.

### Rayon 40

A standard weight machine embroidery thread, this is finer than Rayon 30 but just as successful for tassels. There are 60 colours available on the small 200m (219yd) reels and 341 colours on the

1,000m (1,094yd) cops, including 'ombre' and variegated threads. Ombre thread is a mixture of shades of the same colour while variegated thread is a mixture of different colours.

### Rayon 60
Rayon 60 is even finer than 40 and therefore useful for delicate work. It is marketed as Toledo on cops of 1,500m (1,640yd) in 60 colours.

### Decor
This is a flat, untwisted rayon thread which gives a wonderful, shiny finish to a wooden head. It is available in 40 colours on 190m (207½yd) reels. It can be made into cords, which would give a different finish, and can also be used to make tassel skirts. It does have a tendency to fluff, however, so I would only use it for tassels which will not be handled too much.

### Burmilana
Burmilana is a wool and acrylic mix which looks like a very fine pure wool. The colours are subtle and the feel is good. I use this thread as a wool substitute to get a fine mix of colours easily. It makes good cords and has excellent swingability. Sold on 350m (382½yd) reels, there are 80 colours to choose from.

### Decora
This four-strand embroidery thread is available in 5m (5½yd) lengths in 80 colours. It has a high sheen and is therefore useful for adding highlights to other fibres as well as producing a good, inexpensive tassel on its own.

## Metallic threads
Metallic threads can be very attractive and add an exotic and expensive look to any tassel. The range is enormous. They are not all true metal threads, but are made up of a mix of rayons and metal which gives them strength and pliability. It is advisable to experiment with a small amount of thread to see exactly how pliable it is and whether this is enough for the job you have in mind. Some of the fine ones are too springy and will not hang well when cut. On the other hand, some of the heavier ones hang well but have very little swing. The thread you

choose depends on what type of effect you wish to achieve.

## Heavy threads

All the metallics designed for hand sewing can be used for decorative work. The heavier ones, however, such as Madeira Metallic No. 3 which is softly twisted, can be used in place of decorative cords. Madeira Metallic No. 15, a true metal thread, makes a stiff and heavy skirt. Metallic braids are excellent for covering the wooden heads of tassels and they allow you to stitch into them to add more decoration.

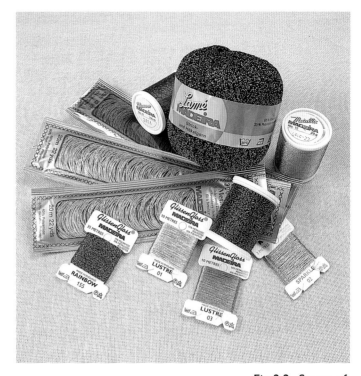

Fig 2.2  Some of the metallic threads on the market: Lustre, Sparkle, Glamour, Lamé, Metallic Gold 15, Rainbow and Metallic 3.

## Glamour

This glittery thread is ideal for making both cords and tassels. It comes in a range of 25 good colours on 100m (109yd) reels.

## Glissengloss

A varied collection of metallic threads is essential when adding decoration to tassels (see Fig 2.2). The Glissengloss range is perfect for this and consists of small amounts of thread wound on to cards – ideal for decorative finishes and for making small tassels suitable for Christmas tree decorations. The range includes the following threads:

- Rainbow, a supertwist 30 thread in a good colour range
- Braid, similar to Madeira Metallic No. 8
- Flash, similar to Madeira Metallic No. 5
- Glimmer, similar to Madeira Metallic No. 15
- Lustre, similar to Madeira Metallic No. 12
- Shimmer, similar to Madeira Metallic No. 6
- Sparkle, similar to Madeira Metallic No. 3
- Sterling, similar to Madeira Metallic No. 40
- Estaz, a chenille-type thread

## Choosing threads

Whether you use thick or thin thread for a particular tassel depends very much on your personal choice. It is always wise to give some thought to the weight and look of the thread in the context of the tassel's purpose: for example tie-backs for large, heavy curtains will need large, heavy tassels. The heavy weight can be achieved by using a thick thread, or masses of fine thread would produce a similar result.

Colour is again a matter of personal choice and taste. If you are trying to match threads with soft furnishings, it is always a good idea to have a sample of the material with you when choosing the thread. No one can carry colour accurately in their head. Try mixing colours to give more interesting results, and look at contrasts as well as at matching threads.

It is advisable to consider texture at the same time as thinking about colour. Amazing results can be obtained by putting a variety of differently textured threads together. Some companies actually sell end-of-line stock as mixed threads in hanks. As well as being economical to buy, they are quick and easy for beginners to use as the threads forming the hank can be wound as a bundle instead of being separated into single threads. I have seen such hanks sold at craft shows in colour-coordinated packs, which can be useful, but you need to be aware that you will probably not find a matching pack at a later date.

It is also necessary to consider whether your chosen thread can be cleaned. If the tassel is to be handled often then the thread should be either washable or dry-cleanable and should not fluff with frequent use. If the tassel is a purely decorative one, any material can be used. An occasional shake will probably be sufficient to keep it clean and free from dust.

**TIP**  Threads which are sold wound on card often have kinks in them when they are removed from the card. The kinks can be removed by dipping your fingers in water and running them down the thread. Allow the thread to dry before you use it.

# Equipment

You do not need a great deal of complicated equipment to make tassels. What you do not already have at home will be readily and inexpensively available from shops or mail order suppliers.

## Basic tools

All the usual sewing requisites are necessary, including sharp scissors (you should keep separate pairs for cutting thread and card), a thimble, and a tape measure. I also keep a ruler and a sharp pencil to hand.

## Needles and pins

You will need several different types of needle, in a variety of sizes: crewel and chenille needles as they are strong, pointed and easy to thread (crewel needles are slimmer than chenille needles); tapestry needles for using when a blunt end is required (especially useful when picking up threads lying on top of others); beading needles or short quilting needles, which can also be used for beading and are easier to thread; and long darning needles, for taking thread through the wooden shapes when binding.

The size of needle depends largely on the thickness of thread being used. If you use a needle with a large eye it will be easy to thread, but if the thread is not particularly thick it will keep pulling out as you work, which is very frustrating. If you use a needle which holds the thread well, you may find it difficult to thread, which can also be very irritating. The needle size is not crucial to the actual making of the tassel, so there is no need to feel bound by my recommendations: use a size which minimizes the frustrations for you.

Glass-headed pins or ordinary dressmaking pins are used as temporary fixings when making some tassels, so it will pay to have a small supply of these to hand.

## Card

A selection of stiff card is essential, as tassels are made by winding the thread around a template of card. If it is difficult or too expensive to obtain stiff card, sticking together layers of card from cereal boxes will provide something of a suitable thickness. The card must be stiff.

If not it will bend with the tension of the thread and so affect the size of the finished tassel.

A craft knife or Stanley knife will be needed for cutting slots in the card used for the various templates.

## Thread winders

A purpose-made thread winder with adjustable pegs (see Fig 2.3) is not essential, but can be useful when making small, all-thread tassels. The distance between the pegs on the winder can be altered to suit the length of the tassel being made. For large amounts of thread you will need very strong pegs, as the winding action does tend to pull the pegs inwards and this can influence the length of the finished tassel. Thread winders are available from suppliers (see page 114), or you can make one yourself from a length of hardwood 6–10mm (¼–⅜in) thick. Drill a line of holes 6mm (¼in) in diameter in the hardwood at 20mm (¾in) intervals. The pegs can be made from dowelling of the right size to achieve a tight fit in the drilled holes. The pegs should be slightly tapered and long enough – 7cm (2¾in) is a good size – to project through the board on one side while providing a generous anchorage for the thread on the other. Tap the pegs into the holes with a hammer. The projection of the pegs on the reverse side of the board enables them to be tapped out easily.

As a simpler alternative to the thread winder described above, you can make a basic winding board from a block of wood, marked with divisions as shown on page 93. This works just as well and is what I normally use.

Fig 2.3 Thread winders with adjustable pegs.

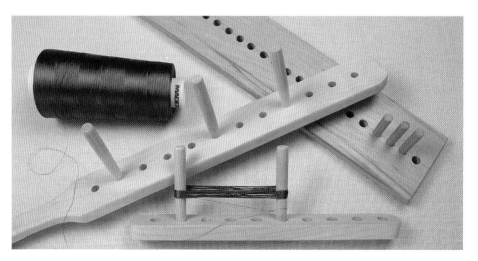

## Cord winding equipment

Cords form an essential part of tassel making, but they can actually be made with very little in the way of tools. Cord winding equipment can vary in sophistication from a pencil and a door handle to a small lathe. Everything you need to know about making cords is included in Chapter 3. Most of the experimental cords I make are simply wound in my hands, because I like to make short lengths in order to see quick results. I then store the cords labelled for reference, and can look back at these when I want to make longer cords for use on a tassel.

## Tassel heads

The solid heads used for making two-part tassels are traditionally shapes turned out of wood. They can be in one piece or made up of small sections which are then strung or wired together to make one head (see Fig 2.4). These are covered with braids or threads and a skirt is attached to the base of the neck. Polished heads are left uncovered to form the decorative head of a tassel and can have the skirt fixed inside rather than attached to the base. These make excellent light pulls (see Fig 2.5).

Unpolished heads for covering are available from various outlets including stockists of Madeira products and some mail order companies (see list of suppliers, page 114). Polished heads can also be ordered from some suppliers, or any woodturner should be able to produce them for you.

**TIP** If you are planning to buy wooden heads for covering vertically (see pages 87–90), make sure that they have a central hole larger than normal, as this will gradually fill up with thread as the head is covered.

Fig 2.4 A variety of shaped, unpolished tassel heads.

Fig 2.5  Polished
tassel heads and
light pulls.

## Beads

Large beads can be used to form a tassel head (instead of a traditional turned shape) and then either covered or left uncovered (see pages 86 and 113). A collection of assorted small beads is also useful for decorating some tassels, and complete skirts can be made from beads as well.

## Thin string

String is invaluable for measuring round tassel necks. It is hard to measure the neck groove on a wooden tassel head accurately without using string, and you will need to know such measurements for the proper fitting of skirts and neck frills.

## Thin wire

Wire is used for anchoring skirts and hanging cords to wooden heads on two-part tassels. I use florist's wire or the single-strand copper wire salvaged from old electrical cables. Fuse wire can also be a great help when beading as it can be made into an improvised and flexible needle; it will also be easier to thread as the eye can be made as big as you wish.

A small pair of pliers is the best tool to use for cutting and bending the wire.

## Adhesives

An adhesive of some sort will be needed when covering a tassel head, but take care in what you choose. I have used both PVA glues and spray adhesives successfully on a variety of threads and so far no ill effects have shown through. The projects later in the book give instructions for using PVA glue only, however, because spray adhesives tend to be very expensive and it is difficult to add extra glue halfway through working without getting it where it is not wanted.

**TIP** I have found it hard to obtain positive reassurance from manufacturers on the real long-term results when bonding different materials together. If you are unsure about a particular adhesive product, then it is always best to test a little on a sample thread beforehand to make sure that no immediate disasters occur.

## Adhesive tape

Sticky tape will be necessary when making some types of tassel (see barber's pole cord on pages 28–9 and mini-tassels on pages 91–5), but be careful to use a tape which is not too sticky, otherwise some of the adhesive will come off on to the thread. Masking tape is ideal, as are other products, such as 3M Magic Tape or Sellotape Invisible, which peel off easily.

CHAPTER 3

# MAKING

# CORDS

C ords feature extensively in tassel making and have a number of purposes. They can be used to make a complete tassel, to cover the head, to decorate a plainly covered head, to bind the neck, to add decoration to a skirt and to make a loop for hanging the tassel. However they are used, they always provide opportunities to introduce extra colour and texture.

It is possible to buy ready-made cords and gimps (thick, soft cords of silk, cotton or wool thread) which can be used for tassel making. Shops selling furnishing fabrics often have a good selection. Decorative cord tied round presents is also worth keeping for use on your tassels. It is much more fun, however, to make your own cords and the results are always far more individual. Before starting work on the tassels themselves, therefore, it is essential to learn how to make cords successfully, and instructions for the different techniques involved are set out and demonstrated in the following pages.

# The principles

A cord can be made from a single thread, but it is often simpler to use a loop of thread as this will help avoid problems to do with the direction in which the thread is twisted (see 'Z and S twists' overleaf). The loop of thread can be one length folded in half with the ends tied together, or two lengths knotted together at each end. A number of threads can also be tied together to form the loop. The loop of thread is twisted, then doubled up and allowed to twist around itself to form the cord.

Cords for binding the neck and for hanging the tassel can vary in weight, even if they are made from the same type of thread. The hanging cord is usually heavier than the neck cord, and this is simply achieved by using more strands of thread. A cord made from two threads, each of six strands, will be thicker and heavier than a cord made from two threads, each of three strands of the same material. Whether it will be exactly twice as heavy, length for length, will depend on the amount of twist in the two cords.

To help with the twisting you will need a slim rod or winding device. The rod can be a pencil, a skewer, a cable knitting needle or even a rolled-up piece of paper. The winding device, if you wish to use one, can be a card winder (a small device sold in embroidery or haberdashery shops for winding thread on to card), a small lathe, a hand drill or a rotary whisk.

## Z and S twists

If you are making cords from more than a single thread, then you will not need to be concerned unduly about whether the thread has an S twist or a Z twist. It is, however, worth sorting out the principles in your mind by trying out the experiments with string detailed on pages 19–21. Not only will this stand you in good stead if you decide to make any cords with a single thread, but it will also clarify all the factors which you need to consider before making any cord.

In the past I have found myself disheartened by conflicting instructions in books concerning Z and S twists of thread. This relates to how the thread is twisted during manufacture, but if you are using a fine machine embroidery thread it is not easy to see the twist unless you use a magnifying glass.

Natural fibres are not very long and not very strong. The fibres are twisted together in order to produce a thread long enough and strong enough to be usable for sewing, knitting, weaving, fishing, towing and all the other uses to which we put thread, string, twine or rope. Man-made fibres can be long and strong without twisting – nylon fishing line for example – but such threads are not very decorative and most manufactured sewing threads are made from twisted fibres.

If the fibres (whether natural, man-made or a mixture) are twisted clockwise during manufacture the resulting thread has an S twist; if the fibres are twisted anti-clockwise the thread has a Z twist (see Fig 3.1). There seems to be little consistency among manufacturers as to the twist characteristics of their threads. Cebelia, for example, has a Z twist, but other DMC threads have an S twist. In the Madeira range there are also many examples of both types of twist.

The following experiments will demonstrate when it is important to know the type of twist on your thread, how to find out which it is, and also when it does not matter. It is worthwhile experimenting in this way with lengths of string before attempting to make cords with more expensive threads by the methods given later in this chapter. For all the experiments I suggest using household string about 2mm (³⁄₃₂in) thick. The string I used had a Z twist. If your string has an S twist (easy to see on string) then the direction for twisting in each experiment should be the opposite of that given in the instructions.

## Experiment 1

Take a 30cm (11¾in) length of string and tie a loop at each end. Put a pencil through each loop and hold one pencil in each hand. Turn the pencil in your right hand in an anti-clockwise direction: you are tightening up the twist already on the string. Give the pencil 30 complete turns. Take the middle point of the string in your teeth and bring the two ends together, holding them in your left hand. Take the folded centre point from your teeth with your right hand and release it. The string will twist back on itself to form a two-ply cord about 14cm (5½in) long. Note that the finished cord has an S twist.

If the string does not form a very smooth cord, try again with another piece of string and this time control the twisting back process by releasing it in stages, starting from the central fold.

## Experiment 2

Repeat Experiment 1, but this time twist the string in a clockwise direction. You will see that the original twist becomes unwound (my string showed itself to be made up of three thinner threads, each of which was made up of five even finer threads which were themselves formed from the shorter elements of the basic fibre). What happens when you bring the two ends together after 30 twists and release the middle is unpredictable. You may get a cord of sorts, but more probably you will find that the individual component threads twist back on each other. Either way the result is distinctly messy.

Fig 3.1 Z and S twists.

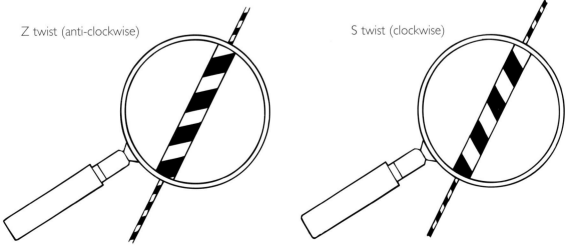

Z twist (anti-clockwise)          S twist (clockwise)

## Experiment 3

Take 60cm (23⅝in) of string and tie the ends together to form a loop. Hold the knot in your left hand. Put a pencil through the loop and hold this in your right hand (you can do this the other way around if you are left-handed). Turn the pencil anti-clockwise, thus twisting the loop of string. Apply about 20 full turns. Note that the twist you are applying is a Z twist. Hold the middle of the twisted loop in your teeth and bring the two ends together, taking them in your left hand. Release the centre of the string from your teeth. The string will twist back on itself to form a four-ply cord about 13cm (5⅛in) long. Note that the finished cord has an S twist.

## Experiment 4

Repeat Experiment 3, but this time twist in a clockwise direction. As the string is tied in a loop the original twist does not become unwound and the two halves of the loop are twisted in an S twist. When the twisted string is released and twists back on itself, the cord which forms is four-ply with a Z twist.

## Experiment 5

Repeat Experiment 3, but use two loops of string. You will be applying a Z twist to four threads which, when they are allowed to twist back on themselves, will form an eight-ply cord with an S twist.

## Experiment 6

Repeat Experiment 3 but use 2m (2yd 6in) of string. It will be necessary to apply more twists (and you will need a helper) so try about 70. This should give you a four-ply, S-twisted cord about 45cm (17¾in) long. Now use this cord and repeat the actions of Experiment 2. The clockwise twisting in this case will add to the twist and so produce an eight-ply cord with a Z twist about 20cm (8in) long.

From these six experiments, various principles become obvious:

1 It is necessary to know the twist direction of the original thread only if you are forming a cord by twisting a single thread. Then it is vital to apply the twist in the same direction as the original.

2 If a cord is to be formed by twisting a loop of thread, then it can be twisted whichever way is most convenient.

3 Cords can be made thicker by adding to the number of threads or loops. Alternatively, cords can be used to make cords.

4 The twisting back process must be controlled by keeping the twisted threads taut before bringing them together, with the fold exactly in the centre, and also by releasing the cord a little at a time, working from the central fold.

5 The ends of the cord must be bound or taped to prevent the twisted cord from unwinding.

The principles established by these experiments with string apply equally to the finer decorative threads used for tassel making. It is not easy to see the twist of a fine machine embroidery thread, but if you are using such a fine thread it is unlikely that you will want to made a cord from a single strand of it. If you are using a loop or loops of thread, which will be more likely, then the experiments above show that the direction of the original twist is not important.

The following methods are intended to introduce you to cord making using threads suitable for use on tassels. I suggest that you do not use very fine threads at this stage: a six-strand embroidery thread will be easy to work and inexpensive.

# Making a short cord

Begin either with a 2m (2yd 6in) length of thread folded in half with the ends bound or knotted together, or with two 1m (1yd) lengths bound or knotted together at both ends.

Loop one end to a suitable fixed point such as a hook, a key in a lock, a door or drawer knob. Place a slim rod through the loop at the other end and apply tension to the threads by moving away from the fixed point (see Fig 3.2).

Twist the rod in a clockwise direction and watch the twist move along the threads (see Fig 3.3).

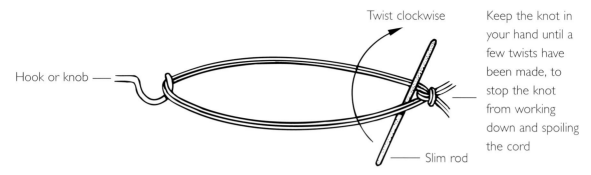

Hook or knob

Twist clockwise

Keep the knot in your hand until a few twists have been made, to stop the knot from working down and spoiling the cord

Slim rod

**Fig 3.2  The threads set up on the rod and fixed point, ready for twisting.**

**Fig 3.3  Twisting with the rod.**

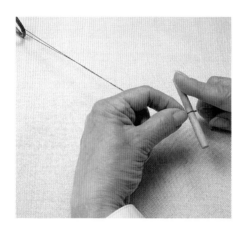

**Fig 3.4  Testing the twist.**

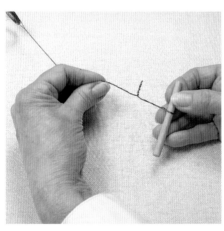

Only experience and practice will help you decide how much twist to apply. The more twist you give the threads, the harder the finished cord will be. It is possible to keep track by counting the number of turns you give the rod, but I have always found this extremely difficult to do unless I am making very short lengths, because I can twist the rod faster than I can count.

The best method of testing the amount of twist you have applied is to hold the thread about 20cm (8in) from the rod with your left hand and allow the cord to relax by moving the right hand towards the left one. The cord will twist automatically back on itself (see Fig 3.4). You

**TIP**  Use the hand that is twisting the rod to keep hold of the knot at the end of the thread as well. The knot has a tendency to move up the thread when the twisting begins and so spoils the cord. Once you have done a few twists the knot should stay put.

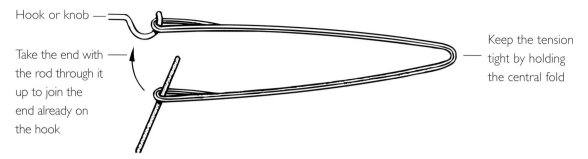

Hook or knob

Take the end with the rod through it up to join the end already on the hook

Keep the tension tight by holding the central fold

Fig 3.5  Folding the twisted thread to make the cord.

can then judge for yourself if enough twist has been applied to suit your purposes.

When you are satisfied that you have applied sufficient twist, you need to fold the thread in half. Take the rod end in your left hand and hold the halfway point of the thread with your right hand (see Fig 3.5). This is where you discover how long your arms are. Take the rod end to the fixed end, using your right hand at the halfway fold to stop the tension from becoming slack. Hook the rod end on to the fixed point and remove the rod (see Fig 3.6).

Keeping the tension up all the time, move your left hand to within 10cm (4in) of your right hand. Hold the thread with your left hand at that point and let go with your right hand. Watch the twist bind the threads together (see Fig 3.7). Use your right hand to stroke the cord gently downwards to remove any kinks that may form.

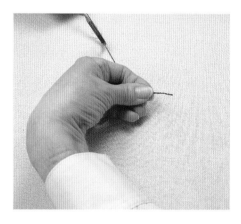

Fig 3.6  Forming the tip of the cord.

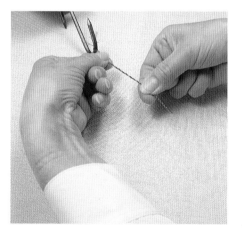

Fig 3.7  Forming the cord.

**TIP**  All the instructions given here are for right-handed people: simply reverse them if you are left-handed.

Fig 3.8 The
finished cord.

**TIP** Whenever you cut
a length of cord from a
longer piece, you must bind
or tie the cut ends together
to stop the threads of the
cord unravelling.

Work up the cord in this way, releasing small lengths by sliding
your left hand a short distance towards the fixed point and easing
kinks with your right hand, until the cord is complete.

When the cord is finished, bind or tie together the two ends at
the fixed point, which will prevent the cord from unravelling
(see Fig 3.8).

Now measure your cord. Having started with 2m (2yd 6in) of
thread folded in half, or two 1m (1yd) lengths, you should end up
with a cord approximately 40cm (15¾in) long, depending on how
much twist you have applied. The more twist you apply, the shorter
the cord. You will soon learn how to adjust the amount of twist
according to the effect you wish to achieve.

# Making very short cords

Very short lengths of cord can be made in your hands, without the need
of a rod or a fixed point to hold one end during the initial twisting.

Take 1.5m (1yd 2 ft) of thread, fold it in half and knot the ends
together. Hold the knotted end in your left hand and put your right hand
index finger through the looped end (or the other way around if you are
left-handed). Hold the thread taut. Twist the thread on your index finger
in a clockwise direction until you have sufficient twist. Fold the thread
in half around a hook or other fixed point (I usually hold the centre of

**TIP** Label each practice cord you make with details of the
type and length of thread so that you can repeat the same
effect at a later date.

the twisted thread in my teeth) and hold the ends in your left hand. Release the thread from the hook (or your teeth) and allow it to twist up into a cord. Smooth the twisted cord with your right hand and tie off the ends held in your left hand (see Fig 3.9).

If you wish to make cords longer than those described above, you will need help either from another person or from mechanical and/or fixed aids. Techniques for making longer cords are explained below.

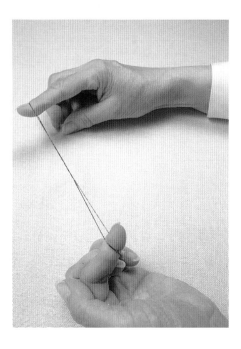

Fig 3.9 A short, hand-held cord.

# Making a longer cord with a helper

First measure out and cut your chosen thread: I suggest starting with a length of 4m (4yd 1ft). Fold the thread in half and knot the ends together.

Fix one end to a hook or other fixed point and put the desired amount of twist on the threads, keeping up the tension all the time. Then ask your helper to find the halfway mark and hold the thread at that point, keeping the tension up while you take your end to the fixed point.

Hold the two ends together while your helper, holding the centre fold of the cord in his/her right hand, takes hold of both threads with the left hand about 10cm (4in) along the cord and lets go with the right hand. Your helper should then stroke the forming cord downwards with his/her right hand to smooth out any kinks. Repeat this process, moving up the cord in stages until it is complete.

**TIP**  If the threads will not stay on the hook or knob being used as a fixed point, tie them on with another thread or an elastic band.

Bind the loose ends, then measure the cord and label it so that you can use it for reference.

Once you and your helper are confident with managing 4m (4yd 1ft) of thread folded in half, try again with 8m (8yd 2ft) of thread. The important thing is to keep the tension up all the time, and to form the cord in small stages, remembering to smooth out the kinks as you go.

## Making long cords with two people twisting

If you are making a cord with more than 8m (8yd 2ft) of thread (a large tassel head may take more than this) then having two people to twist will speed things up. Measure out and tie your lengths of thread as before. Each person holds one end with a rod through it.

Stand facing each other with a chair placed between you to mark the halfway point. With the thread taut, you should each twist your rod in a clockwise direction using your right hand. This adds the twist at a much greater speed than one person can, so will be less time consuming.

When the initial twisting is finished, there are two ways to proceed. You can attach one end to a fixed point in order to free one person to hold the centre point, continuing from there in the same way as described on page 25 in 'Making a longer cord with a helper'. Or you can use the chair as a tensioner while you walk round to combine the two ends (see Fig 3.10). One person should then hold the two ends together while the other removes the end folded round the chair and proceeds as before, working from the folded end in stages to form the cord.

Fig 3.10  The method for making a long cord involving two people and a hook or chair.

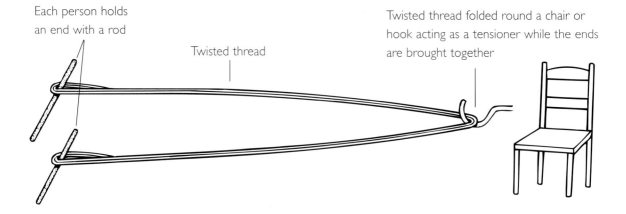

Each person holds an end with a rod

Twisted thread

Twisted thread folded round a chair or hook acting as a tensioner while the ends are brought together

# Alternative methods for long cords

## Making a cord on your own

If you wish to make a long cord and have no helper, you can still use a chair as a halfway tensioner as described above, but one end of the loop of thread must first be attached to a fixed point. Place the chair halfway between the fixed point and the point where you will be standing to apply the twist. When you have twisted the thread, walk round the chair, keeping the tension up, and attach your end of the thread to the fixed point. Remove the thread from round the chair, still keeping the tension up, hold the centre fold and work up the twisted thread in stages to form the cord in the usual way.

I have also made long cords on my own by threading a heavy pair of scissors on to the twisted thread, gathering up the two ends and leaping on to a chair for height, letting the scissors hang down at the centre fold. The weight of the scissors keeps the cord spinning and the tension even, and the result is a very good, smooth cord. The scissors become fixed in the cord at the folded end, of course, so the cord has to be cut to release the scissors and the ends bound or tied together.

## Using a lathe

If you need to make many long lengths of cord, then a small lathe is a useful piece of equipment. Place a hook in the chuck, loop the thread round the hook and tie the ends together. Hold the ends in one hand and switch the lathe on with the other. The twist will be applied in seconds (see Fig 3.11). It is impossible to count the number of twists at this speed, so eye judgement must come into play (or you could use a second timer if you wish to be very precise).

If one person operates the lathe and another holds the thread, it is possible to twist a very long cord in no time at all. If you are working alone, making very long lengths may be less feasible, because you will need to hold the ends of the thread in one hand and control the lathe with the other, while keeping the tension up. If the controls are on the lathe, this will certainly limit the length of cord you can make. A remote control would overcome this problem and some lathes have foot-operated controls.

Fig 3.11 Making a cord using a lathe.

### Using a hand-held drill or whisk

A hand-held drill or one beater in an electric whisk can also be used successfully to help with the twisting of long cords. One end of the loop of thread is attached to a hook in the drill chuck, or to the arm of the whisk, while the other end is looped over a fixed point.

# Colours and textures

Once you are confident of making various lengths of cord successfully, you can start to experiment with different combinations of colours and threads. Exciting results can be achieved by mixing metallic threads with ordinary ones. Thick threads can also be combined with thinner ones. Try out a few different ideas and then label the ones you like with details of thread colours and lengths, for later reference.

The three methods described so far for making cords can be followed for single or mixed colours, but if you wish to have more control over the appearance of mixed threads in a cord, you must use the 'barber's pole' method given below.

# Making a 'barber's pole' cord

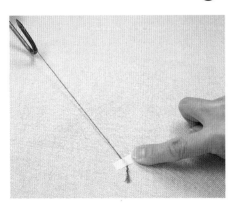

Fig 3.12 The first twisted thread for the barber's pole cord taped down.

**TIP**  A butcher's hook hung over a kitchen drawer makes a good anchorage.

Cut two 50cm (19⅝in) lengths of each of the colours you wish to combine. For your first pieces I suggest using three colours. Tie off the ends of each pair of threads and loop each one on to the same fixed point. This anchorage should be close to a surface on to which the twisted threads can be taped down.

Using a rod, twist one of the colours in a clockwise direction until you are satisfied with the twist. Keeping the tension tight, use masking tape to stick the end of the twisted thread to a surface (see Fig 3.12). Repeat this with all the colours you have cut (see Fig 3.13).

Still keeping the tension tight, release one of the colours at the taped down end and thread the rod through the end. Add all the other colours on to the rod one by one. Then twist the rod in an anti-

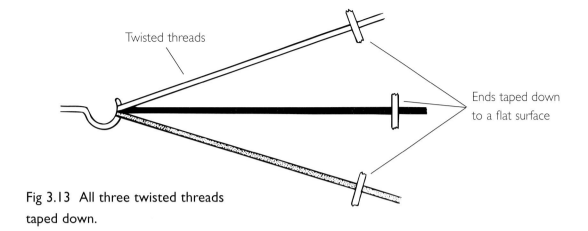

Twisted threads

Ends taped down
to a flat surface

Fig 3.13  All three twisted threads
taped down.

clockwise direction until the barber's pole effect is
as you want it.

Bind together the threads on the rod with
masking tape or thread, still keeping the tension
tight. Tape this bound end to the surface once
again (see Fig 3.14). Bind or tape together the ends
of the cord at the hook end also to complete the
cord before releasing the other end from the
surface (see Fig 3.15).

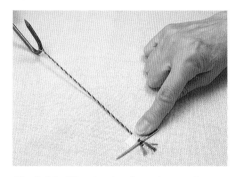

Fig 3.14  The barber's pole cord
taped down after the anti-clockwise
twisting.

Fig 3.15  Finished barber's pole cords.

# CHAPTER 4

# THE BASIC
# ONE-PART TASSEL

T his chapter describes how to make a very basic thread tassel, consisting of a head, a neck and a skirt. A simple tassel of the size and type shown here would be suitable for attaching to the key of a drawer or cabinet, but the principles are the same whatever size of tassel you are making. The method of winding thread on to a card template and then tying it to make a tassel is not only applicable to the 'one-part' tassels shown here and in Chapter 5. It is also a method which will be adapted later in the book to make decorative neck frills and to wind the skirts for 'two-part' tassels.

The plain tassel shown in this chapter to demonstrate the technique was made from Madeira Rayon 30 and Cotton Perle. Advice on choosing your own threads is given in Chapter 2, and the materials list on page 33 gives alternatives. The colours, of course, are entirely a matter of personal choice, as they are for all the projects in this book.

Instead of making a plain tassel you can use two threads of contrasting colours to create different effects. The two threads need not be of the same type. Using two threads together throughout the winding process will give a tassel with mixed colours. Alternatively, changing colours halfway through winding produces a tassel with a contrasting centre. Fig 4.1 shows four different tassels – one plain, one with mixed threads, one with metallic thread and one with a contrasting centre.

The finished tassel in this project is 7cm (2¾in) long. The skirt is two-thirds of the total length of the tassel, and the head and neck make up the remaining third (see Fig 4.2). This ratio of two-thirds to one-third creates a well-proportioned tassel, but there is no hard and fast rule: it is largely down to personal taste.

The size of the card template on which the thread is wound determines the size of the finished tassel. The depth of the template must be 1cm (⅜in)

Fig 4.1  Four one-part tassels, with plain thread, mixed thread, metallic thread and a different centre.

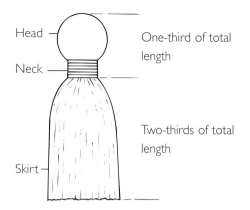

Head

Neck

Skirt

One-third of total length

Two-thirds of total length

**Fig 4.2 The parts of a tassel.**

greater than the final length of the tassel, to allow for tying, cutting and trimming. The width of the template depends on the thickness of the thread being used: the thicker the thread, the wider the template must be. For my 7cm (2¾in) tassel made from fine thread I used a template 8cm deep and 9cm wide (3⅛ x 3½in). If I had been using wool, I would have made the template 12cm (4¾in) wide to accommodate the thicker thread.

# Materials and equipment

All the materials and equipment needed for this basic thread tassel are shown in Fig 4.3.

**Fig 4.3 The materials needed for making a basic tassel.**

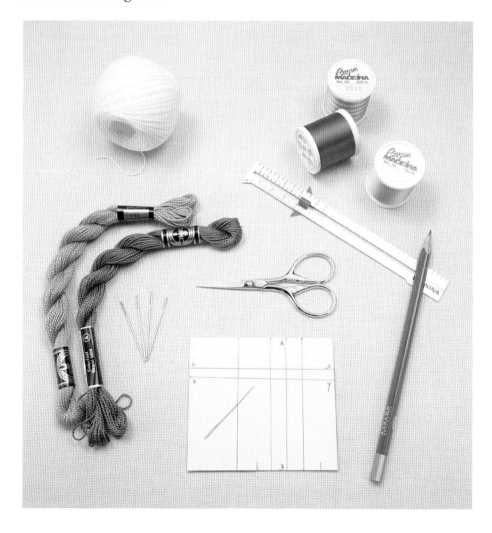

## Tassel thread
- 200m (219yd) reel of Madeira Rayon 40

*or*

- 150m (164yd) reel of Madeira Rayon 30 (Rayon 30 is thicker than Rayon 40 so there is less on the reel to give the same bulk)

*plus*

- 1 skein or ball of matching Cotton Perle 5

## Tying thread
- Six-strand embroidery thread

*or*

- Cotton Perle 12

*or*

- Cebelia 20

*or*

- Any thread of a contrasting colour

## Other requirements
- Stiff card, 8 x 9cm (3⅛ x 3½in)
- Ruler
- HB pencil
- Scissors for cutting card
- Scissors for cutting thread
- Tapestry needle size 20

# Method

## Preparing the template

Begin by marking up the card template (see Fig 4.4 for the guidelines).

Use a sharp pencil to mark the card vertically into three equal sections: in this case each section will be 3cm (1⅛in) wide. Label the line on the right A–B as shown in Fig 4.4.

> **TIP**  The marked up template shown in Fig 4.4 is the correct way round for a right-handed person. If you are left-handed, mark everything the other way round, so that the shaded holding area is on the right-hand end.

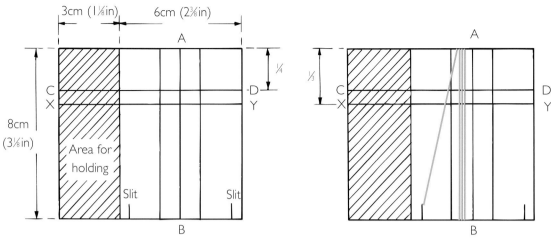

Fig 4.4  The template card.

Fig 4.5  The thread anchored in the slit ready for winding.

Next draw a horizontal line a quarter of the way down the card: 2cm (¾in) in this case. Draw a second line in the same position on the reverse side of the card. Label both these lines C–D as shown. This line marks the top of the neck.

Draw a second horizontal line one-third of the way down from the top of the template and label it X–Y. This line shows the position of the bottom of the neck.

The shaded area in Fig 4.4 indicates the part of the template you will be holding, to prevent your fingers getting in the way when you are winding the thread.

To act as a guide while you are winding, mark two further lines, 1cm (⅜in) either side of the line labelled A–B. Finally cut two 1cm (⅜in) slits on the bottom edge of the card, in the positions shown in Fig 4.4. These will help anchor the thread at certain points during the making of the tassel.

## Winding the thread

Anchor the end of the thread (the Madeira Rayon 30 or 40) in one of the slits on the template card (see Fig 4.5). Use the left-hand slit if you are right-handed, or the right-hand slit if you are left-handed.

> **TIP**  Place the reel of thread in a plastic or paper bag while winding. This will stop the reel from rolling around and will keep the thread clean.

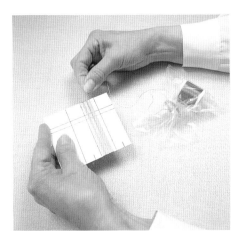

Fig 4.6  Winding the tassel.

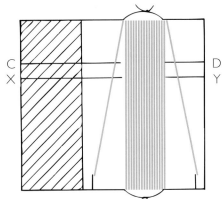

Fig 4.7  Tying the top and bottom.

Begin winding the thread evenly round the card, from top to bottom (as shown in Fig 4.5). Keep the bulk of the thread as close as possible to the line marked A–B and within the two guiding lines marked on either side of it (see Fig 4.6). Wind fairly tightly, but not so tightly as to bend the card. Bending the card will affect the size of the tassel. Continue until you have used up all the thread on the reel.

Use one of the slits to anchor the end of the thread when you have finished winding, or if you need to interrupt the winding for any reason. New, differently coloured threads can be introduced at any stage simply by anchoring them in a slit and continuing with the winding.

## Tying top and bottom

Thread the tapestry needle with a 15cm (6in) length of your tying thread. Put the needle through the centre of the wound thread, between the thread and the card. Pull the thread through, move it up and tie the ends loosely together at the top of the template (see Fig 4.7). Repeat this with another 15cm (6in) length of tying thread at the bottom of the template (see Fig 4.8).

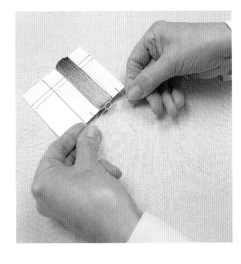

Fig 4.8  The top and bottom of the tassel after tying.

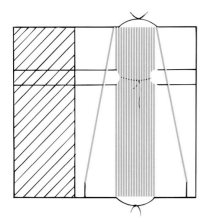

Fig 4.9  Tying the neck.

## Tying the neck

The lines on the template labelled C–D and X–Y (see Fig 4.4) mark the top and bottom of the tassel's neck. Thread the tapestry needle with another 15cm (6in) length of tying thread and pass this between the thread and the card. This time tie it tightly round the threads between lines C–D and X–Y (see Fig 4.9).

Turn the card over and tie the threads on the other side in the same way.

## Removing the tassel from the card

Before doing anything else at this stage, it is vital to free the threads anchored in the slits. If you forget to do this and try to remove the template, you will pull the threads and distort the tassel.

Once the threads are free, the template can be removed. Carefully bend the card a little and ease the tassel off. The tying threads will keep the wound threads neatly together.

## Adding the hanging cord or thread

Thread the tapestry needle with 20cm (8in) of Cotton Perle 5. Push the needle through the centre of the top of the head, where the original tying thread sits. Remove the tying thread and tie the hanging thread tightly in its place, with the knot on top of the tassel (see Fig 4.10). If you are using a cord for hanging the tassel instead of plain thread, attach it in the same way.

Fig 4.10 Attaching the hanging thread.

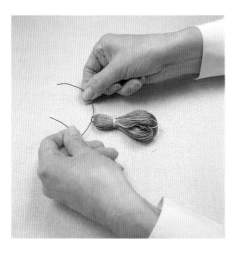

**TIP**  All threads are easier to secure in a knot if they are slightly damp. Dip your fingers in a saucer of water, moisten the thread with your fingers and then tie the knot.

Leave the ends loose: the hanging cord or thread is used to tie the tassel to the key or other item to be decorated.

## Binding the neck

Use the Cotton Perle 5 to secure and bind the neck of the tassel.

First trim off the ends from the two tying threads which you placed round the neck of the tassel earlier, just leaving the knots. Thread the tapestry needle with 1m (1yd) of Cotton Perle 5 and tie a knot in the end. As the tassel is still divided at the neck, you can begin from the inside, passing the needle through to the outside, then back – about 3mm (⅛in) from where the needle came out – and right through to the other side of the neck (see Fig 4.11). This will bring the two sides of the tassel together, securing the knot on the Cotton Perle thread inside the neck. Leaving the thread loose, remove the needle.

Now wrap the Cotton Perle tightly round the area shown in Fig 4.4 (i.e. the area between lines C–D and X–Y) until the neck is bound to your satisfaction. The original tying thread will be covered up in the final binding process. Bear in mind that the head and the neck should make up one-third of the total length of the tassel. Wind the threads neatly side by side, working up and down the neck and finishing at the top.

Fig 4.11 Passing the needle through the neck to combine the two sides before binding.

Secure the end of the Cotton Perle by rethreading the needle and passing it through the neck from top left to bottom right (see Fig 4.12) and then from front to back, right through the tassel. Pull the thread up tight. Pass the needle through the neck once again from top to bottom, pull the thread very tight and trim the ends as close as possible to the neck.

Fig 4.12 Using a needle and thread to finish off the bound neck.

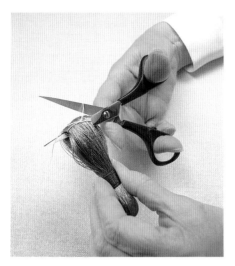

Fig 4.13  Cutting the skirt.

Fig 4.14  Squeezing water out of the skirt.

**TIP**  One drop of washing-up liquid added to 285ml (½pt) of water acts as a wetting agent and enables the thread to absorb the water more easily.

## Cutting the skirt

By now the skirt threads, having been handled, will probably have twisted, so use the tying thread at the bottom of the tassel as a guide when cutting the skirt.

Using a sharp pair of scissors, insert one blade through the bottom of the tassel. Pull the tassel tight on the scissors while holding the neck in your other hand (see Fig 4.13). Cut as cleanly as you can through all the threads, checking that all the loops have been cut. Do not worry at this stage if the ends are not level. This will be sorted out last of all.

## Straightening the tassel

Immediately after cutting, the threads of the skirt will be splayed and curled. Some people like to leave their tassels like this, but it is more usual to have the threads hanging straight.

It is easy to straighten the threads using cold water, but if you suspect that the thread you have used is not colour-fast, it would be wise to test a small sample amount beforehand, to check that none of the dye runs out when the thread is immersed in water. This applies particularly to hand-dyed threads. Most manufactured threads are colour-fast and will cause no problems.

When you are satisfied that there is no danger of dye bleeding from the tassel, dip the skirt in cold water and then squeeze out as much as you can. The best way to do this is to grip the neck firmly between the thumb and first finger of one hand and squeeze the water from the skirt with the first and second fingers of your other hand, working from the top to the bottom (see Fig 4.14).

Hang the tassel up and leave it to dry. If the skirt is still not completely straight when the tassel has dried, repeat the process.

## Finishing off

The bottom of the skirt will not be perfectly level yet. When the tassel has been straightened and dried, hold it by the top in your right hand and place the skirt between the first and second fingers of your left hand. Run your fingers down towards the bottom of the skirt. You should now be holding the bottom edge of the skirt between the first and second fingers of your left hand,

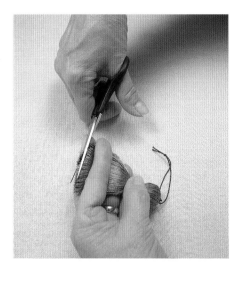

Fig 4.15 Trimming the skirt.

ready to be trimmed, with the main part of the tassel lying in the palm of your left hand (see Fig 4.15). Naturally, if you are left-handed, you will need to do this with your right hand, so that you can wield the scissors with your left hand.

Trim the threads with very sharp scissors, in short, snipping cuts, until you think the skirt is level. Do this slowly and cut off just a little at a time: you can easily cut off a little more, but you cannot put back what you have already cut off.

Give the tassel a quarter-turn and repeat the trimming process. Turn and trim until you are certain that the skirt is perfectly level. Give the tassel a shake and hang it up for 24 hours. You may find that a final trim is necessary once the threads have had a chance to settle down (see Fig 4.16).

Fig 4.16 The finished tassel.

**TIP** Tassels need to be kept clean and tidy so they look their best. A tassel which has become untidy through use can be smartened up by dipping in cold water, squeezing, drying and trimming as described above.

# CHAPTER 5

# DECORATING

# ONE-PART TASSELS

T here are many ways to add interest to a simple tassel. Included here are seven projects setting out different ideas for embellishing a basic one-part tassel such as the one described in Chapter 4, using frills, beads and jewellery findings to create a variety of effects.

All the projects involve sewing different kinds of decoration on to the head and/or neck of the tassel. It makes sense to use standard methods for starting and finishing these sewing tasks each time, so instructions for these are given separately at the beginning rather than being repeated for each project. You can refer back to these initial instructions whenever necessary.

# General instructions

## To begin working

Thread the needle and tie a knot at the end of the thread. Push the needle into the centre of the neck or head of the tassel – whichever is nearest to the position where you want to begin (see Fig 5.1). Pull the thread through so that the knot disappears inside the tassel and does not pull out (see Fig 5.2). If it pulls straight out, tie a bigger knot. Once the knot is inside the tassel, take the needle through the tassel again, pulling the thread tightly so that the knot becomes securely buried (see Fig 5.3).

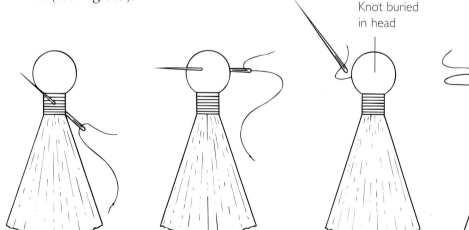

Fig 5.1  Pushing the needle and thread into the centre of the neck or head of the tassel.

Fig 5.2  Pulling the thread through so that the knot goes inside the tassel.

Fig 5.3  Taking the needle back through the tassel to secure the knot.

## To finish working

Take the needle through the tassel at the point where you have been working and pull it out at the other side. Repeat this three times, making sure that the threads are buried in the thick part of the tassel head or neck.

## To join threads while working

If you need to replace a thread while binding the neck, follow the procedures described above, first for finishing (to end the old thread), then for beginning work (to start the new thread).

If the thread has to be replaced when working a decorative stitch, such as the buttonhole stitching for the mob cap (see pages 47–51), more care has to be taken with the tension so that the stitching appears to be continuous. Take the needle through the head of the tassel where the next stitch should be and pull gently until the stitch lies in position (see Fig 5.4). Take the needle back into the head and bring it out at the neck, pulling gently to avoid disturbing the last stitch (see Fig 5.5). Then proceed as normal for finishing, taking care not to pull too hard, or the decorative stitching will be distorted. The threads are finished at the neck, so they will be made secure when the neck is bound in the finishing process. Anchor the new thread at the neck in the normal way for starting work, and bring the needle up in place for the next stitch so that the finished decorative stitching will seem continuous (see Fig 5.6).

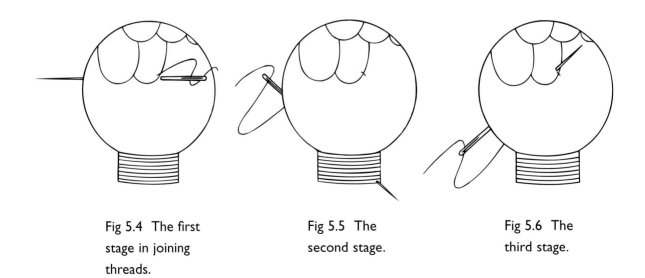

Fig 5.4  The first stage in joining threads.

Fig 5.5  The second stage.

Fig 5.6  The third stage.

## 🌿 PROJECT 🌿

# NECK FRILL

## Materials and equipment

- Basic one-part tassel made from Rayon 30 or Rayon 40, with tying threads in place at the top, bottom and neck (i.e. prepared to the stage of removing the card as described on page 36)
- 1 card of Rainbow thread for the neck frill (or other thread of your choice)
- Thin string 20cm (8in) long
- Stiff card twice as wide as your intended frill and 7cm (2¾in) longer than the distance round the neck of the tassel (see step 2 below)
- Crewel needle sized to suit your chosen frill thread (size 10 is correct for use with Rayon 40, Sticku or Rainbow)
- 4 glass-headed or dressmaking pins

## Method

1 Remove 10m (11yd) of Rainbow thread from the card. Wind this on to another card and set aside for the hanging cord and for stitching the frill.

2 To make a frill of the right size you need a correctly proportioned template on to which you wind the thread (see Fig 5.7). The width of the card should be twice the width of the required frill. For the basic tassel being used for this project, the frill will be 1cm (⅜in) wide, so the template must be 2cm (¾in) wide.

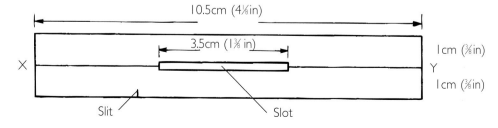

10.5cm (4⅛in)

3.5cm (1⅜in)

X

Y

1cm (⅜in)

1cm (⅜in)

Slit

Slot

Fig 5.7 The frill template.

The template's length should be the distance round the neck of the tassel plus 7cm (2¾in). To measure the neck, take the piece of thin string and tie it tightly round the neck of the tassel. Cut the string off and measure the part which was tied round the neck. My neck measured 3.5cm (1⅜in), so my template was 10.5cm (4⅛in) long. Your tassel neck may be a different size, so measure it and adjust the size of your template accordingly.

3 Mark the length of the tassel neck in the centre of the card along the line X–Y shown in Fig 5.7. Mark a line 2mm (³⁄₃₂in) from the centre line on each side of it. Cut out this area with a craft knife, leaving a slot in the template. Also cut a slit to anchor the thread when you begin winding (see Fig 5.8).

Fig 5.8 The position of the thread over the slot on the template during winding.

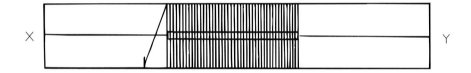

4 Anchor the thread in the slit, then begin to wind the thread round the template from the beginning of the slot. Wind evenly and firmly across the card until you reach the end of the slot (see Fig 5.8), then wind the thread back in the opposite direction. Keep winding backwards and forwards in the same way until all the thread from the Rainbow card is used up (see Fig 5.9). Anchor the thread in the slit at the end of winding.

5 Thread the crewel needle with 1m (1yd) of the Rainbow thread from the card you wound right at the start. Double the thread and knot the ends together. Check that the wound threads of the frill are all contained within the length of the slot on the template. Now begin an overlapping backstitch by bringing the needle through the slot, from the back of the card to the front, 2mm (³⁄₃₂in)

**TIP**  Do not wind the thread too tightly, or the card will bend inwards and cause the frill to be too narrow in the middle.

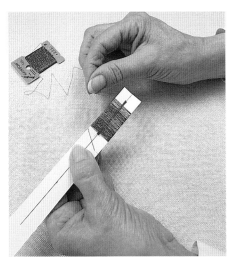

Fig 5.9  Winding the neck frill.

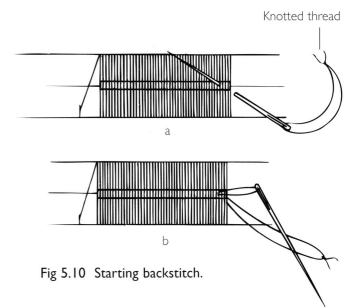

Knotted thread

a

b

Fig 5.10  Starting backstitch.

from the right-hand edge (or the other edge if you are left-handed) of the threads (see Fig 5.10a). Pull the needle through, then take it back between the knotted sewing threads (see Fig 5.10b), pulling the thread up tight to secure it.

Overlapping backstitch (see Fig 5.11) means that the threads will be connected all the way through, which will stop the frill stretching when it is removed from the card. Continue stitching the threads together through the slot until the process is complete. Leave the needle attached at this stage. (The completed frill should fit the neck of the tassel perfectly, as the length of the slot on the template should be equal to the distance round the neck.)

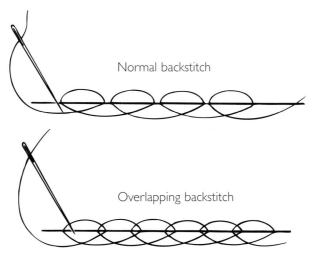

Normal backstitch

Overlapping backstitch

Fig 5.11  Overlapping backstitch (side view).

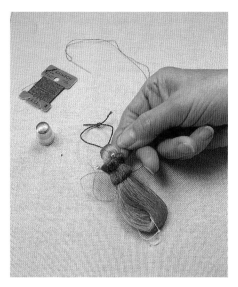

Fig 5.12 The completed frill, before being removed from the template.

Fig 5.13 The frill pinned in place on the tassel.

6 To remove the frill, cut off the template at the end of the slot opposite to the one where the needle is still attached (see Fig 5.12). Take great care not to cut the threads. Bend the card so that the frill slides off easily (remember to free the thread anchored in the slit).

7 Pin the frill to the neck of the tassel with four pins, taking care not to stretch it (see Fig 5.13).

8 Stitch the frill to the tassel by backstitching over the row of overlapping backstitch and into the neck of the tassel (see Figs 5.14 and 5.15). Use the needle and thread which you left attached to the frill.

9 The frill can be left as loops, or the loops can be cut to give a more pompom-like appearance.

10 Make a hanging cord (see Chapter 3) from the remaining 9m (9yd 2½ft)

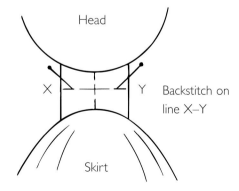

Fig 5.14 Stitching the frill to the neck.

Fig 5.15  The frill fixed to the neck.

Fig 5.16  The completed tassel and neck frill.

of Rainbow thread. This will give you 12 lengths of thread, each measuring 75cm (29⅝in): use two groups of six threads each to make a strong hanging cord.

11 Attach the hanging cord, remove the tying threads and cut, straighten and trim the skirt as described in Chapter 4, pages 38–9. The completed tassel is shown in Fig 5.16.

## ❦ PROJECT ❦
# MOB CAP

# Materials and equipment

- Basic one-part tassel made from Rayon 30 or 40 without a hanging cord but with neck and skirt tying threads in place
- 1 skein of Cotton Perle 5
- Tapestry needle size 20
- Chenille needle size 20
- 8 glass-headed or dressmaking pins

# Method

**1** Thread the tapestry needle with a 50cm (19⅝in) length of Cotton Perle thread.

**2** Anchor the thread in the tassel head (see 'To begin working' on page 41).

**3** Bring the needle out at the top of the head, just off the centre point.

**4** Work one chain stitch (see Fig 5.17) right on the top of the tassel (see Fig 5.18).

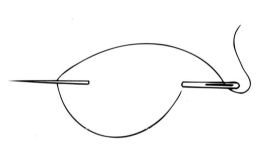

Fig 5.17  The first stitch at the top of the tassel: chain stitch.

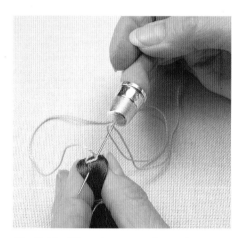

Fig 5.18  The chain stitch in place.

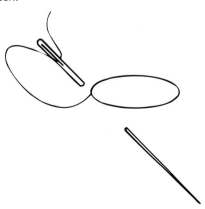

Fig 5.19  Push the needle into the tassel and bring it out just below the chain stitch.

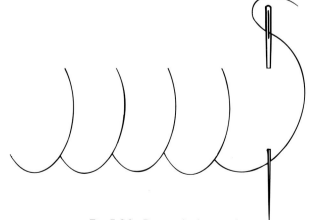

Fig 5.20  Buttonhole stitch.

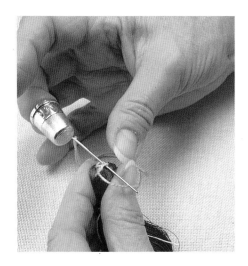

Fig 5.21  The first buttonhole
stitches on the tassel.

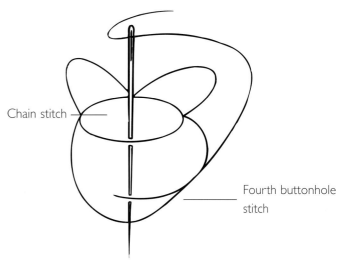

Chain stitch

Fourth buttonhole
stitch

Fig 5.22  The first four buttonhole stitches
in place around the chain stitch.

5 Take the needle through the tassel head and come out just
below the chain stitch (see Fig 5.19).

6 Work a buttonhole stitch (see Fig 5.20) into the chain stitch
without going through the tassel head (see Fig 5.21). This is
called detached buttonhole stitch: it will hang from the chain stitch
and further rows will form a net over the tassel head.

7 Work three more buttonhole stitches into the chain stitch,
moving round the head so that the last stitch is next to the first
(there should be four buttonhole stitches in all – see Fig 5.22).

8 Continue by working two buttonhole
stitches into the first buttonhole stitch,
again without going into the tassel head.

9 Now work two more stitches into
the second buttonhole stitch.
Continue to work round the first four
stitches in this way, putting two new
stitches into each one. You will finish with
eight stitches round the head (see Fig 5.23).

Fig 5.23  Adding
further
buttonhole
stitches: view of
the top of the
tassel head.

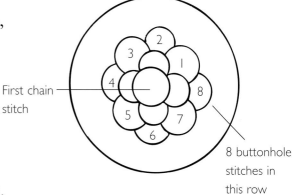

First chain
stitch

8 buttonhole
stitches in
this row

10 Now work one buttonhole stitch into each of the previous eight stitches, which should take you about halfway down from the top of the tassel to the neck (see Fig 5.24). It may help to push eight pins into the tassel to keep the mob cap in position as you work downwards.

11 Repeat this last row of single stitches until you reach the neck. This will make a rather stretchy mob cap.

12 When you reach the neck, slip stitch the last row of buttonhole stitching to the neck using the thread remaining in the needle (see Fig 5.25).

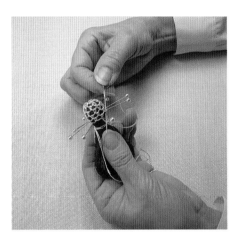

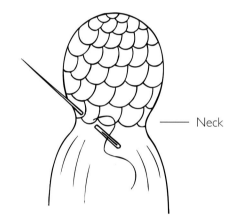

Neck

Fig 5.24 The half-completed mob cap, pinned to keep it in position.

Fig 5.25 Slip stitch to attach the last row of buttonhole stitches to the neck.

13 Bind the neck with 1m (1yd) of the Cotton Perle thread, as described in Chapter 4, page 37, then finish off the thread to complete the neck (see Fig 5.26).

14 The hanging cord is best added at the end, as it will get in your way if it is already in place while you are stitching the mob cap. Make the cord from 1m (1yd) of Cotton Perle thread folded in half (see Chapter 3). Attach it to the tassel by threading it on to the size 20 chenille needle and taking it through the chain stitch, picking up some of the tassel threads underneath the chain stitch at the same time. Tie the cord to make a hanging loop.

15 Finish the tassel by cutting, straightening and trimming the skirt. Fig 5.27 shows the completed mob cap tassel.

Fig 5.26  The completed bound neck.

Fig 5.27  The finished mob cap tassel.

## ❦ PROJECT ❦

# BEADED NECK

## Materials and equipment

- Basic one-part tassel made from Rayon 30 or 40 with the tying threads still in place
- Small packet of seed beads (beads can be bought in packets, on threads, or loose)
- Fine nylon thread or the thread used for making the tassel (or a thin cord which will fit through both the needle eye and the beads)
- Thread for hanging cord
- Beading needle size 10

**TIP**  The thread used for sewing on the beads does not have to be an exact match to the tassel or the beads, as it will not be visible once the beads are in place. There is no need to change the colour of the thread if you change the colour of the beads.

# Method

1 Thread the beading needle with a length of your chosen thread. Anchor the thread to the tassel neck (see page 41), bringing the needle out at the base of the neck, at the point marked X in Fig 5.28.

2 Thread three beads on to the needle and thread.

3 Take the needle into the neck of the tassel as if you are forming a running stitch, at the point marked Y in Fig 5.28. The distance between X and Y must be enough to accommodate the three beads. Bring the needle out again at the point marked Z in Fig 5.28. The distance between Y and Z should be enough to accommodate the next three beads (see Fig 5.29). Judging these spaces accurately will come with practice, but it is better if the space is too large than too small to avoid the danger of scrunching up the beads.

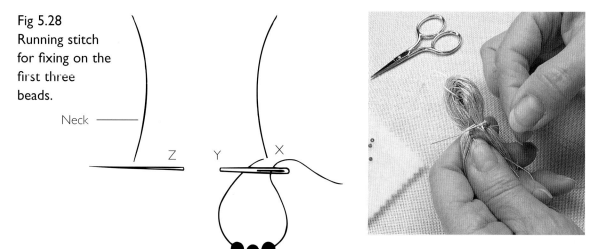

Fig 5.28
Running stitch
for fixing on the
first three
beads.

Neck ———

Z    Y    X

Fig 5.29 The first three beads in place on the tassel neck.

**TIP** If you have difficulty threading a beading needle, any needle will do as long as it will pass through the beads. I have sometimes used a fine wire bent in half instead of a needle.

4 Pull the thread tight and thread on three more beads.

5 Take the needle into the head of the tassel again, just in front of the last bead, and bring it up ahead, allowing space for the next three beads. You are forming a backstitch, but adding the three beads in the middle of the stitch (see Fig 5.30).

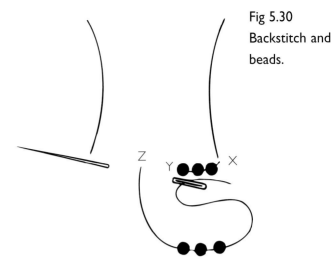

Fig 5.30 Backstitch and beads.

6 Work round the neck in this way. When you get to the last set of beads, you may not need to use three to fill the remaining space, so just thread on the number you require. Complete the row by bringing the needle out again between the first set of beads on the same row (see Fig 5.31).

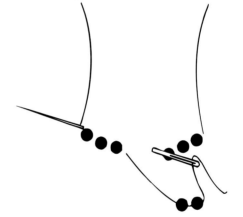

Fig 5.31 Fitting the last set of beads into the row.

7 Next thread the beading needle back through all the beads in that row (see Fig 5.32). The needle is very flexible, but you may still have to bring it out every few beads and take it back in again at the same place to work round the circle. This will bring all the beads in the row into line, as they will be held in tension by the same thread. At this stage, remove the original tying thread from the neck if it shows.

Fig 5.32 Running the beading needle and thread back through the whole first row of beads.

Fig 5.33 The finished tassel with beaded neck.

8 Add another row of beads immediately above the first one, using the same number of beads for each row and adding them on in twos or threes. Repeat the rows until you are satisfied with the look and depth of the neck. Finish the thread off securely (see page 42).

9 Make and tie on a hanging cord, then cut, straighten and trim the skirt. The completed tassel is shown in Fig 5.33.

# Alternative beaded necks

You need not use the same size and colour of beads for the whole neck: try using larger beads for the top and bottom rows, or mixing different coloured beads. If an even number of beads is used for each row, then a spiral pattern can be worked out by dividing them into equal sections (see Fig 5.34).

To make a tassel with a long and elegant beaded neck, rather than the short one demonstrated above, simply start to bead the neck as above and continue beading upwards, keeping the tension tight and even (the head of the tassel will, of course, become smaller if you choose to have a longer neck). There is no hard and fast rule as to how long a neck should be: the length you find pleasing is the right one. A frill (see pages 43–7) can be added beneath the beads (see Fig 5.35).

**TIP** To prevent beads from rolling or spilling, place a few at a time on a piece of felt or soft material and use them from there.

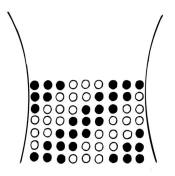

Fig 5.34 Forming the beads into a spiral pattern for the neck.

Fig 5.35 Tassels with long beaded necks and frills.

🦋 PROJECT 🦋

# BEADED HEAD

## Materials and equipment

- Basic one-part tassel made from Rayon 30 or 40, with tying threads at the top, neck and skirt
- Selection of beads – pick a variety of colours and sizes (I used seed beads and a mixture of others 4–8mm ($\frac{5}{32}$–$\frac{5}{16}$in) in diameter)
- Thread for attaching the beads (fine nylon thread or the thread used for making the tassel)
- Beading needle size 10
- Thread to make hanging cord
- Decorative cord to bind the neck

## Method

1 Start in the centre top of the head and add one bead (see page 41 for instructions on starting work and page 52 for sewing on the first bead).

2 Add a row of beads immediately round the first bead, then take the needle back through them all to line them up evenly.

3 Continue to work the rows of beads down the head (see Fig 5.36), varying the number of beads per row to allow for the shape of the head. Finish off the thread securely when the head is complete.

4 Prepare the hanging cord. If the top bead on the head is large enough, add the hanging cord through the bead. If the bead is not large enough to allow this, then the hanging cord will need to be fixed on through the top of the tassel itself.

**TIP** The same technique is used for beading the head as for the neck in the previous project. However, if you are using beads of varied sizes, it is better to work with one bead at a time rather than three.

5 Bind the neck below the beads with a decorative cord, then cut, straighten and trim the skirt. The completed tassel is shown in Fig 5.37.

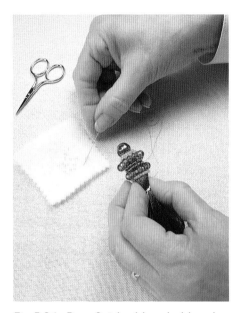

Fig 5.36  Part-finished beaded head.

Fig 5.37  Completed tassel with beaded head.

## ⚘ PROJECT ⚘

# BEADED SKIRT

## Materials and equipment

- Basic one-part tassel made from Rayon 30 or 40, with hanging cord, tying thread at the neck and the skirt cut and straightened
- Selection of beads of different sizes, up to 6mm (¼in) in diameter
- Decorative thread for making cords on which to hang the beads
- Thread for making the neck cord
- Chenille needle size 20
- Beading needle size 10
- Glass-headed or dressmaking pins

# Method

1. Prepare the cords to take the beads. For this project you will need eight cords. Each should measure roughly the length of the skirt plus 10cm (4in).

2. Tie a knot at the cut end of each of the prepared cords so that the knot is positioned 1cm (⅜in) above the level of the bottom of the skirt when the looped end of the cord is level with the neck of the tassel (see Fig 5.38). Do not cut any excess cord off at this stage (see Fig 5.39). When the tassel is complete, the ends below the knot are cut level with the bottom of the skirt.

3. Thread the beads on to the cords (see Fig 5.40) and set on one side.

4. Make another cord from 1m (1yd) of thread folded in half, then thread the chenille needle with this cord and secure it at the top of the skirt (see page 41).

5. The beaded cords have knots in their cut ends, so the other end is the looped one (see Chapter 3). Take the beaded cords and thread their looped ends on to the cord you have attached to the tassel.

**TIP** It is easier to make the beaded cords level with the skirt if the tassel has already been cut, straightened and trimmed. This is what I have done for this project. Of course, you can choose to make the beaded cords either longer or shorter than the skirt.

Fig 5.38  Tying a knot into a prepared cord.

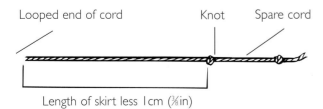

Looped end of cord    Knot    Spare cord

Length of skirt less 1cm (⅜in)

Fig 5.39  The position of the knots on the cord.

Fig 5.40  Threading the beads on to the cord.

**TIP**   Adding beads to the skirt of a tassel helps add weight and swing as well as extra colour.

6 Wind this cord round the top of the skirt, spacing the beaded cords evenly round it. Use pins to hold them in position for the time being (see Fig 5.41).

7 Now pull the cord tightly into the neck of the tassel, wrap it round three times and secure the end.

8 Cut off the excess cord below the knots holding the beads, level with the bottom of the skirt. The finished tassel is shown in Fig 5.42.

Fig 5.41  The beaded cords pinned in place round the skirt.

Fig 5.42  The finished tassel with beaded skirt.

<h1 style="text-align:center">⚓ PROJECT ⚓</h1>

<h1 style="text-align:center">SPIDER'S WEB HEAD</h1>

# Materials and equipment

- Basic one-part tassel made from Rayon 30 or 40, with tying threads in place at the top, neck and skirt
- Thick thread in a contrasting colour (I used six-strand embroidery thread for this example)
- Smooth thread, either matching or contrasting with the tassel (a fine handmade cord or a Perle thread are both easy to work and I used Cotton Perle 5 for this example)
- Chenille needle size 20
- Tapestry needle size 20 (or one suitable for your chosen smooth thread)
- Hanging cord (I made mine from 1m (1yd) of Cotton Perle 5)

# Method

1 Thread the chenille needle with the thick thread (I used six-strand embroidery thread) and secure this at the tassel head, bringing the needle out at the top of the neck (point A in Fig 5.43).

2 Take the thread over the top of the tassel and push the needle in again directly opposite the point where it first came out

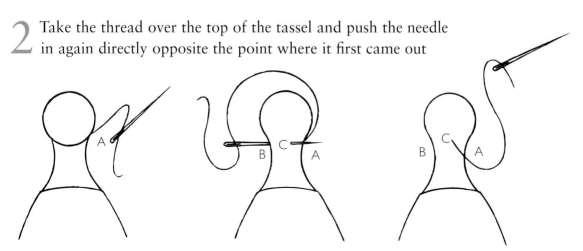

Fig 5.43 Laying the foundation for the web.

Fig 5.44 The
web struts being
put in place.

(point B in Fig 5.43). Bring it out at the point marked C in
Fig 5.43, i.e. halfway between points A and B (see Fig 5.44).

3 Repeat this process until you have eight strands of thread
going over the top of the tassel (see Figs 5.45 and 5.46). These
threads will cover the top tying threads.

4 Secure the thread in the neck. You will see that you have now
produced a framework for a spider's web by putting in the
basic strands or struts. These will be covered by the top thread and
so will not show through when the tassel is complete.

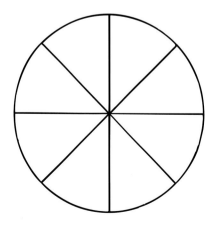

Fig 5.45 The eight struts or strands:
view from the top of the tassel head.

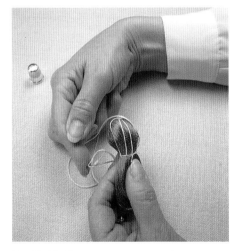

Fig 5.46 Strut preparation being
completed.

5 Now thread the tapestry needle with your chosen smooth thread (I used Cotton Perle 5). Knot the end and secure the thread in the head of the tassel, bringing the needle out at the centre of the top.

6 Take the needle under two of the web strands, without picking up any of the tassel threads. Pull the thread through gently (see Fig 5.47a).

7 Take the needle back over the last web strand you picked up, go under it again, and then under the next strand. Pull the thread through gently, again making sure that you are only picking up the frame of the web and not the threads of the tassel head itself (see Fig 5.47b).

8 Repeat this process around the head, until you are back where you started.

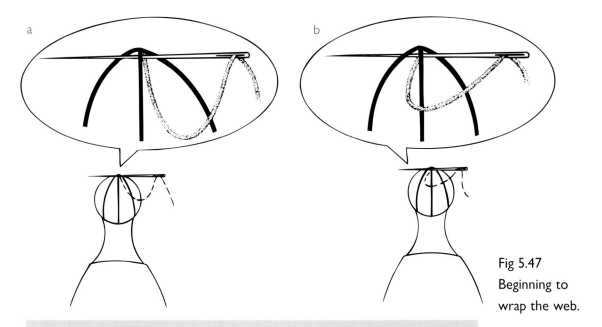

a  b

Fig 5.47
Beginning to
wrap the web.

**TIP**  If you do pick up some tassel threads but do not notice until too late, cut the tassel threads where they show on the web and pull them very carefully out of the tassel after you have cut the skirt.

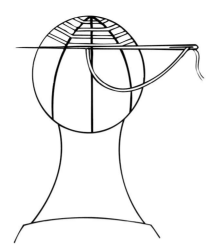

Fig 5.48  The web wrapping in progress.

Fig 5.49  The half-completed web.

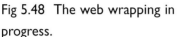

9 Now work another row in the same way, making your way down the head (see Figs 5.48 and 5.49). It is vital to keep the tension even as you work down the web framework. If you pull too hard, the struts of the web will be forced out of line. If you leave the tension too loose, you will end up with uneven loops of thread round the struts. As you work round the bowl of the head, however, be aware of the shape and allow the tension to ease to give a rounded effect. If you want a straighter look, pull harder to tighten the tension.

Fig 5.50  The completed spider's web tassel.

10 At the bottom of the web, bind the neck with the Cotton Perle thread and secure the end of the thread.

11 Make your hanging cord if you have not already done so and attach it by stitching it through the web structure in the centre of the head. Secure it with a knot over the web structure.

12 Finally cut, straighten and trim the skirt. The finished tassel is shown in Fig 5.50.

> **TIP** A 'spider's web' makes a very neat finish to the head of a tassel. It does need some careful preparation, but once that is done, the rest is easy.

## ❧ PROJECT ❧
# JEWELLERY FINDING HEAD

## Materials and equipment

- 1 card of Rainbow or Sterling thread
- 1 small, conical earring finding (see Fig 5.51)
- Beading needle size 10 or crewel needle size 10
- Card template for winding a 5cm (2in) tassel (see pages 33–4)

Fig 5.51 Various jewellery findings suitable for tassel making.

## Method

1 Prepare a hanging cord using 1m (1yd) of Rainbow or Sterling thread, doubled over twice (this will make a shorter and fatter cord). Put the cord to one side.

2 Thread the needle with another 1m (1yd) of the thread, then use the rest of the thread on the card to wind round the template for the 5cm (2in) tassel.

3 Secure the top, bottom and neck of the tassel with tying threads as described for the basic one-part tassel on pages 35–6, then remove the tassel carefully from the template card.

4 Take the needle and thread, secure the thread in the neck of the tassel (see page 41) and bind the neck with half the thread, about 50cm (19⅝in). Secure the thread again, but do not cut it or remove the needle.

5 Remove the top tying thread and place the conical earring finding over the top of the tassel. Hold it firmly in position, take up the needle and thread again, and slip stitch the cap to the tassel (see Fig 5.52). Secure the thread and cut it off (see Fig 5.53).

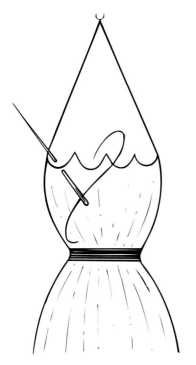

Fig 5.52  Slip stitching the cap to the tassel head.

Fig 5.53  The finding in place on the tassel head.

6 Now thread the cord through the hole at the top of the finding and tie it to make a hanging loop of the length you require (see Fig 5.54).

7 Cut the skirt, trim and straighten. The finished tassel is shown in Fig 5.55, along with other tassels made with larger jewellery findings. The smaller ones are ideal to use as Christmas tree decorations.

Fig 5.54  Attaching the hanging loop through the top of the finding.

Fig 5.55  Finished tassels with jewellery finding caps.

# Further decorative ideas for necks

Some of the projects in this chapter have provided ideas for decorating the neck of a tassel. There are many more possibilities to be found with a little imagination.

Fig 5.56  Two tassels with necks bound with ombre thread.

Try using more elaborate, decorative threads and cords, or make cords from braid for a fatter cord with an interesting texture.

Narrow florist's or parcel ribbon can be split and bound round the neck. Tie the ends in a bow, curl the ends and allow them to hang down.

Ombre threads can be used to great advantage (see page 8), as their colours are so well spaced out. Wrap the neck with the thread, keeping the first colour all in the same place. When the colour changes, move up the neck and wrap in the same place until the colour changes again (see Fig 5.56). Variegated threads can also be used, but their colour changes are not necessarily so uniformly spaced as the ombre range.

# CHAPTER 6

# THE BASIC
# TWO-PART TASSEL

B y now you should be confident with the method for making a one-part thread tassel, and with the various techniques involved in different types of decoration. Once you have mastered the principles of basic tassel making, branching out with alternative ideas should prove straightforward. Whether you are making a small one-part tassel or an elaborate two-part one with a covered head and highly decorative skirt, the basic methods are the same.

This chapter sets out two ways to make a two-part tassel by attaching the skirt to a shaped wooden head. The first gives the basic method of covering the shaped head and making and attaching the skirt. The second is simply a variation on this, but introduces more variety in the covering for the head. Chapter 7 contains projects with further decorative ideas for tassels with covered shaped heads.

The shapes for tassel heads are usually turned from wood. They have a hole through the centre so that the hanging cord can be secured, and a groove round the base where the skirt is attached. It is also possible to make up a head from several small components, using the central hole to link them together (see Fig 6.1). Tassel heads are available in some craft shops, or they can be obtained direct from suppliers (see page 114).

These shapes are covered with threads or braids to make decorative tassel heads. The threads used as the covering can then be used as a base on which to stitch further decoration such as beads, wired hand-made flowers, needlelace flowers, sequins and so on.

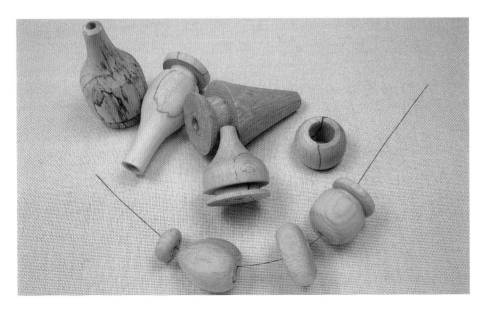

Fig 6.1 A selection of uncovered wooden tassel heads.

## ❧ PROJECT ❧

# TASSEL WITH COVERED HEAD

## Materials and equipment

- Shaped wooden head (choose a simple shape for your first tassel, as the more complex ones are not so easy to cover – see Figs 6.1 and 6.2)
- 625m (683yd) cop of Sticku 30 for the skirt (or a thread of your choice)
- Cords or braids to match your chosen skirt thread (I used Cotton Perle 5 as a cord in this project)
- White PVA adhesive (you will also need a small brush)
- Crewel needle size 10
- Florist's wire or single-strand copper wire
- Bendy straw, or skewer, or a piece of 6mm (¼in) dowelling
- Card for the skirt template (see Method for size instructions)
- Small amount of clingfilm
- Small pair of pliers
- 1 bead slightly larger than the hole in the tassel head

Fig 6.2  The differences between a simple shape which is easy to cover and a more complicated shape which demands more skill to cover well.

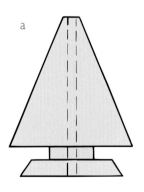

a

Conical shaped head which is easy to cover

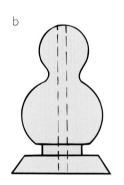

b

More complex shape, but gentle curves are easy to cover

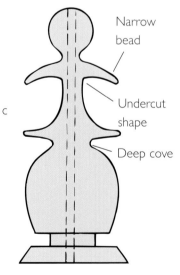

c

Narrow bead

Undercut shape

Deep cove

Such a complicated shape is difficult to cover

# Method

**1** Wrap the bendy straw (or skewer/dowelling) in clingfilm and place it through the centre of the wooden head. This gives you something to hold while applying the glue so that the glue does not get transferred to your fingers. The clingfilm will help the straw grip the sides of the hole.

**2** Cover the head with a thin film of adhesive and allow it to dry (see Fig 6.3). This will seal the wood and means that the second layer of glue will remain wet and on the surface of the wood long enough for you to apply the decoration. If it does dry because you are slow in applying the decoration, more glue can be added at any time with a small brush.

**3** If you have not made your cords beforehand, prepare them while the first layer of glue is drying. The cords should be made to the longest length with which you can work comfortably. They can be joined as you bind the head, so it is not essential to make one long cord.

**4** Once the first layer of glue has dried, keep the head on the straw and apply the second layer thinly and evenly.

**TIP** If the straw or skewer is smaller than the hole through the centre of the head, wrap round more clingfilm until you have a good fit.

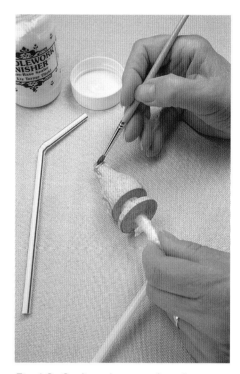

Fig 6.3 Sealing the wooden shape with a first layer of glue.

**TIP** If you feel you need to know exactly how much cord to make, wrap the shaped head round with string which roughly matches the size of the cords you plan to make. Measure how much string it takes and this will be the amount of cord you require. It is so easy to make a cord, however (see Chapter 3), that it is not essential to have an exact measurement.

**Fig 6.4** Starting to wrap the cord round the head.

**TIP**  If the tassel head is more than 8cm (3⅛in) long, apply the second layer of glue initially to the top two-thirds only. Work the cord or braid on to this part first, then apply the second layer of glue to the bottom third. This will mean that you do not have to rush in order to reach the bottom before the glue dries.

Tuck the first 2cm (¾in) of cord into the central hole

Wind cord round the head, pressing into the glue

**Fig 6.5**  The end of the cord tucked into the top hole.

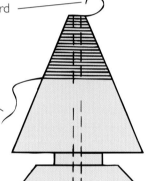

5 While the glue is still wet, begin to apply the cord to the top. Tuck the first 2cm (¾in) of cord into the central hole, then start to press the cord on to the head around the hole (see Figs 6.4 and 6.5). The straw will help you to turn the head as you apply the cord.

6 Continue to press the cord round the head, winding downwards until you reach the neck. Make sure that no space is left between the cord as you wind and press. If you run out of cord, stick the last 1cm (⅜in) down as shown in Fig 6.6. Then begin a new cord by sticking the first 1cm (⅜in) down as shown and continue with the new cord exactly where you left off with the old one. The stuck-down ends will be hidden as you work over them (see Fig 6.7).

New thread laid alongside the original then wound on

Original thread

**Fig 6.6** Joining lengths of cord.

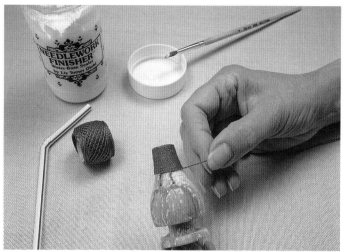

**Fig 6.7** Covering the end of the old cord with the new length of cord.

**Fig 6.8** Wrapping the neck and securing the end of the cord.

7 When you reach the neck groove, glue the cord in to cover it, but stop short of the bottom lip of the shape. Remove the straw at this stage. Make sure that the final end is secure by stitching it into place with a fine thread (see Fig 6.8).

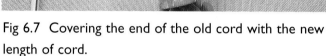

Holding area

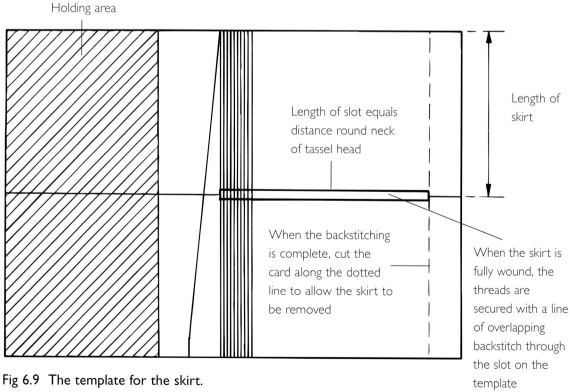

Length of skirt

Length of slot equals distance round neck of tassel head

When the backstitching is complete, cut the card along the dotted line to allow the skirt to be removed

When the skirt is fully wound, the threads are secured with a line of overlapping backstitch through the slot on the template

**Fig 6.9** The template for the skirt.

Fig 6.10  The thread anchored on to the card template for the skirt.

Fig 6.11  Winding the thread for the skirt.

8 Measure the distance round the neck groove with a length of string and note the measurement down.

9 Make the template for the skirt, following the method given for making the neck frill template on pages 43–4 (see Figs 6.9 and 6.10). The length of the slot on the template card should be equal to the distance round the neck, as before. The width of the card should be equal to twice the length of the skirt.

10 Wrap the skirt thread round the template card, keeping within the length of the slot, and secure the final end in a slit cut in the card (see Fig 6.11).

11 Use overlapping backstitch (in the same way as for making the neck frill, see pages 44–5) through the slot in the template to secure the threads of the skirt (see Figs 6.9 and 6.12).

**TIP**  You can use a sewing machine instead of backstitching at this point. Machine through the slot in the card twice, once in each direction, using a straight stitch.

Fig 6.12  Using overlapping backstitch to secure the threads of the skirt.

Fig 6.13  Removing the skirt from the card template.

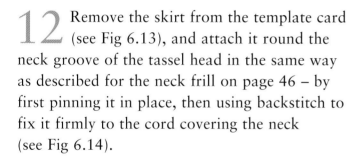

12 Remove the skirt from the template card (see Fig 6.13), and attach it round the neck groove of the tassel head in the same way as described for the neck frill on page 46 – by first pinning it in place, then using backstitch to fix it firmly to the cord covering the neck (see Fig 6.14).

13 Now you need to make the hanging cord if you have not already done so. Hanging cords are usually thicker than the cord used for binding the shaped head, and are often ornate. For the hanging cord shown in this project I used 2m (2yd 6in) of Cotton Perle 5 folded into four. Knot or stitch the ends of the finished cord together to make a loop.

14 Cut a piece of wire to use for attaching the cord to the head. The wire needs to measure the length of the tassel head plus 10cm (4in). Make a hook at one end of the wire, put it

Fig 6.14  Pinning and stitching the skirt to the base of the covered head.

Fig 6.15  The tassel at this stage in the process, with the hanging loop and wire ready to be attached.

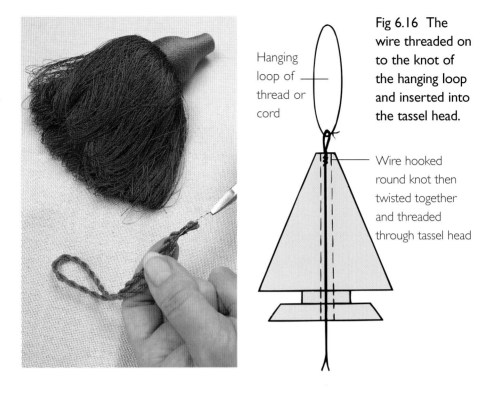

Hanging loop of thread or cord

Fig 6.16  The wire threaded on to the knot of the hanging loop and inserted into the tassel head.

Wire hooked round knot then twisted together and threaded through tassel head

through the knotted or stitched end of the hanging loop and twist the wire firmly together (see Figs 6.15 and 6.16).

15 Thread the wire through the centre of the head so that it protrudes at the bottom (see Fig 6.16), then pull it firmly so that the knot on the cord loop goes into the top of the head. You may have to use pliers to achieve this (see Fig 6.17).

Fig 6.17  Pulling the wire through the head of the tassel (the knot should disappear into the head).

**TIP**  Two-part tassels are not so easy to hold in your hand for trimming because of the extra bulk of the wooden head. After the first trim it is best to hang the tassel from a hook, so that you have one hand completely free to control the skirt when trimming again.

16 Thread the bead on to the wire and push it firmly up against the bottom of the central hole. Wrap the wire round the top of the bead and trim off any excess (see Figs 6.18 and 6.19).

17 Cut, trim and straighten the skirt (see pages 38–9), then trim again if necessary when dry. The finished tassel is shown in Fig 6.20.

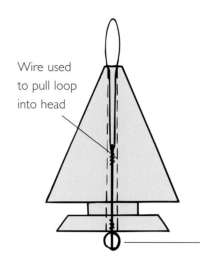

Fig 6.18 Securing the end of the wire, knot and part of the hanging loop in the central hole.

Wire used to pull loop into head

Wire secured by threading through bead then bending round over top of bead

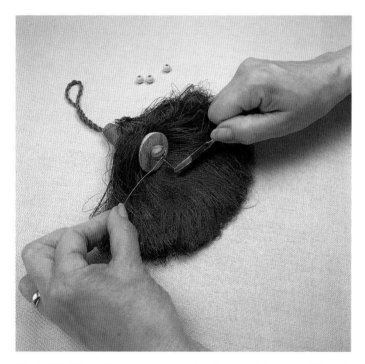

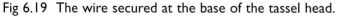

Fig 6.19 The wire secured at the base of the tassel head.

Fig 6.20 The finished two-part tassel.

## ❧ PROJECT ❧

# COVERED HEAD WITH VARIED BINDING

## Materials and equipment

- Small shaped wooden head (pick a simple one again, as for the previous project)
- 2 skeins of Cotton Perle 3 or 5, each of a different colour, for the tassel head
- 6 skeins of Renaissance wool, 2 each of 3 different colours, for the skirt (the precise amount required will depend on the size of the head)
- White PVA adhesive
- Chenille needle size 20
- Florist's wire or single-strand copper wire
- Bendy straw, skewer or piece of 6mm (¼in) dowelling
- Card for the skirt template
- Small amount of clingfilm
- Small pair of pliers

## Method

1 Follow steps 1, 2 and 4 from the previous project (see page 69).

2 Using one colour of the Cotton Perle 3, glue it to the very top of the head and start winding it round. Work about one-third of the way down the head – the precise distance should be dictated by the proportions of the shape you have picked (see Fig 6.21).

3 Add the second Cotton Perle colour by sticking down the end – about 1cm (⅜in) – at 90° to the wound thread, then continue to wrap the shape with the two colours side by side (see Fig 6.21). Cover the 1cm (⅜in) tail as you go.

Start binding with one colour, tucking about 2cm (¾in) into the top hole

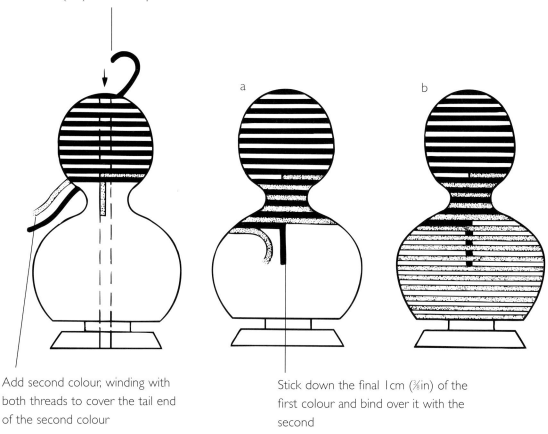

Add second colour, winding with both threads to cover the tail end of the second colour

Stick down the final 1cm (⅜in) of the first colour and bind over it with the second

**Fig 6.21 Binding the first thread on to the head.**

**Fig 6.22 Adding a second colour to the binding.**

4 When you reach a point approximately two-thirds of the way down the head, cut off the first thread colour and stick down the last 1cm (⅜in) at 90° to the wound thread (see Fig 6.22a). Continue with the single, second thread, covering the final tail of the first colour, working down to the neck (see Fig 6.22b). Secure the thread by gluing it into the neck groove.

5 Make a template for the skirt as described in step 9 of the previous project (page 72).

**TIP** Keep the balls of thread in a plastic bag to keep them clean and under control. Wind both threads together, running them smoothly between your fingers to keep them parallel.

6 There are two possible methods for winding the skirt with the three different colours of Renaissance thread:

(a) Wind on all three colours simultaneously, so the skirt will end up multi-coloured throughout, *or*

(b) Wind on each colour separately to create contrasting blocks of colour within the tassel. Start, for example, with the darkest colour, covering the whole of the slot on the template card, then do the same with the middle colour, then the lightest. Cover the area of the slot as evenly as possible with each colour for the best effect.

When you have finished winding, secure the end of the thread in a slit in the card.

7 Complete the skirt and attach to the tassel head as set out in steps 11 and 12 of the previous project (see pages 72–3).

8 Now make two hanging cords from the Cotton Perle thread, one long enough to use as a hanging loop, the other to fit round the neck as decoration (this one should be long enough to go right round the neck and be tied in a bow).

9 Attach the hanging loop using a piece of wire as described in steps 13–16 in the previous project (see pages 73–5).

10 Stitch the neck cord in place over the top of the skirt, then tie a small bow in the cord and leave the ends hanging down.

11 Cut, trim and straighten the skirt of the tassel to finish it off (see Fig 6.23).

Fig 6.23 The finished tassel with varied head binding and skirt.

# CHAPTER 7

# DECORATING

# TWO-PART TASSELS

Chapter 6 introduced the method for putting together a simple two-part tassel. Here, the use of shaped heads is developed further. Five projects demonstrate more complex decorative techniques for covering the heads and enhancing the skirts of the tassels – showing how to use several shapes to make a head, how to wrap the head to achieve different effects, and how to apply decoration to both head and skirt.

### ❧ PROJECT ❧

# WOOL TASSEL WITH MULTI-SHAPE HEAD

This tassel has a head made up of several smaller component shapes (see Fig 7.1). This allows you to make up a shape exactly as you like, using turned wooden shapes, beads, or even shapes you have made yourself from a modelling clay such as Fimo. All the individual shapes must have a hole through the middle, and the bottom shape needs a groove round its base (or neck) to take the skirt. The component pieces are wrapped individually with thread or cord, so this is an opportunity to add variety by wrapping them in different directions and/or with different threads.

**TIP** Make sure that the shapes which are to be wrapped vertically have larger than normal central holes (see Method overleaf).

Fig 7.1 The components of the multi-shape head.

# Materials and equipment

- 5 small hanks of Paterna wool or crewel wool – you could stick to one colour, but I used three (1 hank of a dark shade, and 2 each of medium and light shades)
- Individual shapes for the head – I used 4 shapes to make a head measuring 8cm (3⅛in) holding a skirt of 14cm (5½in)
- Chenille needle size 20
- White PVA adhesive
- Small pliers
- Florist's or single-strand copper wire
- Card for skirt template

# Method

1 Coat the wooden shapes with an initial layer of glue to seal the wood, and leave to dry (see page 69).

2 While the glue is drying, make the cords. I made three cords, each from 2m (2yd 6in) of single-strand Paterna wool. I used two of these for the larger horizontally covered shape, and one for the smaller. For the vertically wrapped shapes I used five 2m (2yd 6in) lengths of single-strand Paterna wool, folded in half on the needle.

3 Select the individual shapes which you would like to cover horizontally (in the same way as for the first project in Chapter 6, 'Tassel with covered head', on pages 68–75). The easiest shapes to cover in this way are those with straight or sloping sides (see Fig 7.2) rather than the more rounded ones (see Fig 7.3). Use the straighter ones as the top and bottom shapes when putting the tassel head together (see Fig 7.1).

**TIP** If you are using crewel wool, it would be advisable to make it into cords before use as it is so fine. If you are using Paterna wool, you can use it as it is, or split it into strands and make cords if you prefer.

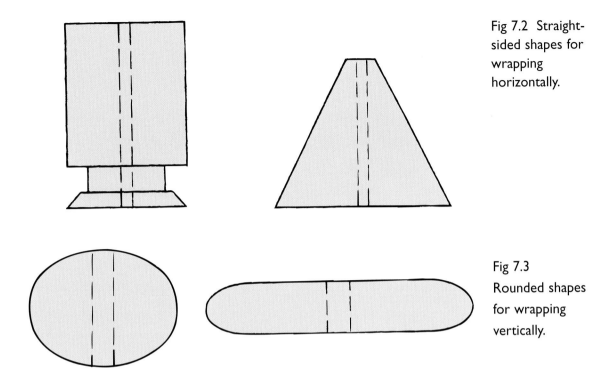

Fig 7.2 Straight-sided shapes for wrapping horizontally.

Fig 7.3 Rounded shapes for wrapping vertically.

4 Take one of these straight-sided shapes at a time and give it a second coat of glue. Then wrap it with the wool (either plain thread or cords, see above) as described in Chapter 6 on pages 70–1. Glue and wrap each shape in turn.

5 Once you have dealt with the horizontally wrapped shapes, turn to the rounded ones, which are to be wrapped vertically. This calls for an entirely different method of wrapping which needs no second layer of glue: the thread is held in place by the tension of the wrapping. First thread the chenille needle with thread (a single strand, doubled up then knotted) and push this through the centre hole of one rounded shape. Then take the needle through the knotted end of the thread and pull tight. The thread will now be fastened firmly round the shape. Make sure that the join is hidden inside the shape (see Fig 7.4).

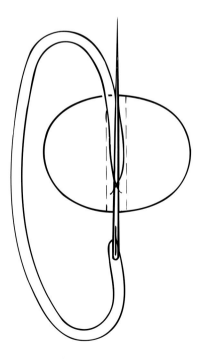

Fig 7.4 Starting to wrap vertically.

Fig 7.5 A
vertically
wrapped shape.

6 Wrap the thread round the shape and take the needle through the centre again, gently pulling the thread tight. Repeat this process and you will see that the shape is being wrapped neatly and vertically. Continue until the shape is completely covered (see Fig 7.5), then secure the thread by stitching it into the threads inside the shape. Cut off the end of the thread. Cover each rounded shape in the same way.

7 Now make two cords, each from 1m (1yd) of wool folded twice. Loop and knot one to be used as a hanging cord. The other will be needed for neatening and decoration.

8 Cut a length of wire to hold the head shapes together. The wire should measure the total length of the head plus 10cm (4in). Make a hook at one end of the wire, put it through the knotted end of the loop of hanging cord and twist the wire firmly together.

9 Thread the wire through the shapes for the head, starting with the top and working down in the correct order (see Fig 7.6). Pull the hanging loop into the top shape (using pliers for extra grip if necessary) and secure the wire tightly at the bottom by bending it at right-angles to the central hole (see Fig 7.7). Alternatively, you could secure the wire round a bead as described on page 75. Cut off any excess wire.

10 Make a card template for the skirt in the same way as described on pages 71–2. The size of the slot will depend on the size of the component shape at the bottom of your tassel head.

**TIP** When winding on the wool, use the slits at the bottom of the template to anchor the start and finish of each new hank or length of thread. If you are using mixed colours, wind them together to get a good mixture throughout the skirt.

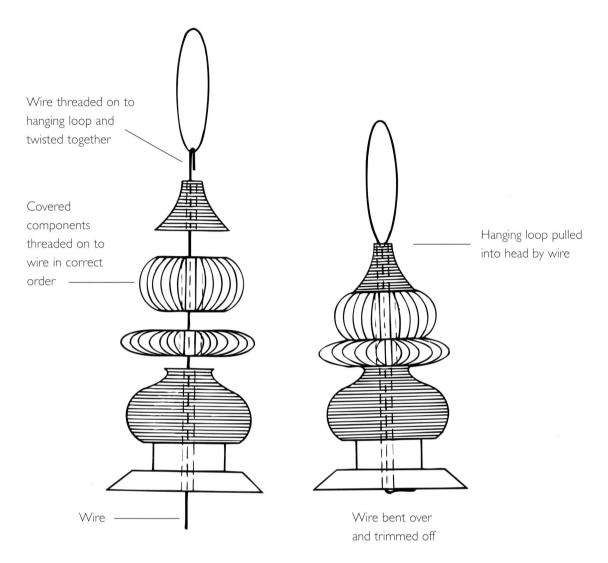

Wire threaded on to
hanging loop and
twisted together

Covered
components
threaded on to
wire in correct
order

Wire

Hanging loop pulled
into head by wire

Wire bent over
and trimmed off

Fig 7.6  The order for putting the head
together.

Fig 7.7  The components on the wire.

11 Wind all the remaining wool on to the template, keeping
the threads within the confines of the slot on the card.
Then secure the threads of the skirt using overlapping backstitch
through the centre of the template (see pages 45 and 73). Remove
the skirt carefully from the template card.

12 Attach the skirt to the base of the head by pinning and
backstitching it to the threads or cords wound round the
neck (see pages 46 and 73).

13 Cut the skirt threads in the usual way (see pages 38–9).

14 If the wool you have used is plied (Paterna wool is plied, but crewel wool is not) you will need to separate the plied strands in order to bulk up the skirt. This can be done by putting a tapestry needle into each plied thread and gently pulling out one strand (see Fig 7.8). This will loosen the other strands in the ply and they should separate easily. This may seem a laborious task at first, but it can be quite relaxing and it is something you can do while watching television. It will certainly seem worth it when you end up with a beautifully plump skirt.

15 Trim the tassel once more, damping to straighten if necessary.

16 Neaten the top of the skirt by tying the second decorative cord round it, leaving the ends of the bow to hang down. The finished tassel is shown in Fig 7.9.

Fig 7.8 Separating strands of plied wool to bulk up the skirt.

Fig 7.9 The completed tassel.

## ❦ PROJECT ❦

# COMPLETE TASSEL HEAD WITH VERTICAL WRAPPING

In the previous project, two components from a multi-shape head were chosen to be wrapped vertically. They were easy to cover because of their rounded, bead-like shape. This project explains how to apply vertical wrapping to a complete shaped head with concave and convex curves. Pick a shape which does not have excessively exaggerated angles, and make sure that the central hole is wider than usual, to accommodate the thread which will be taken through it many times. You will need to choose a fine thread if you are making cords for winding, or use the thread straight from the reel. Fine wool is best used in single strands.

You could use individual shapes and work each one separately instead, as in the previous project, but using a single shape will produce a smoother effect.

## Materials and equipment

- Shaped wooden head with curved edges, no more than 6cm (2⅜in) high
- Five 10m (11yd) hanks of Anchor Tapisserie wool (I used a hank of one colour for the vertical wrapping, a hank of a different colour for both horizontal wrapping and cords, and the rest was all used for the skirt)
- Darning needle
- Chenille needle size 20
- Florist's wire or single-strand copper wire
- Small pliers
- Card template for skirt

**TIP**    Wool works well for vertical wrapping because it has plenty of give or stretch in it.

# Method

1 Cut two 1.5m (1yd 2ft) lengths of wool from the hank of the colour to be used for the horizontal wrapping in step 6. Fold each length in half and make each one into a cord. One cord will form a hanging loop and the other will be used to decorate the top of the skirt.

2 Thread the darning needle with the colour of wool you wish to use for the vertical wrapping, double it and knot the ends together.

3 Put the needle and thread through the central hole of the shaped head, from the top to the bottom, leaving the knot hanging out at the top. Then put the needle through the loop at the knotted end of the thread and pull up firmly, easing the threads round so that the knot is hidden inside the shape (see Fig 7.10).

4 Now push the needle into the hole at the bottom of the shape and out at the top. Pull the thread up very gently, making sure that the threads on the outside of the shape lie side by side (see Fig 7.11) and over your fingers (see Fig 7.12). This allows some slack in the thread for when you add the horizontal wrapping in step 6.

5 Repeat the process described in step 4 until you have completely covered the outside of the shape (see Fig 7.13). Finish off the thread by stitching it inside the tassel head.

Fig 7.10
Attaching the
winding thread
to the shape.

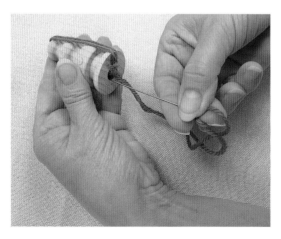

**TIP** If you need to start a new thread during the wrapping process, begin again with step 3, then carry on with the wrapping, keeping the threads side by side.

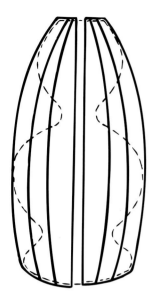

Fig 7.11  The way the threads lie after vertical wrapping.

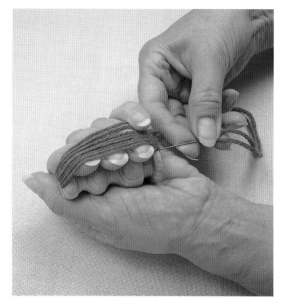

Fig 7.12  The vertical wrapping in progress.

6 The wrapped threads will have altered the appearance of the head, making straight lines where there were concave curves. It is now necessary to bind the head horizontally, in the concave parts of the head, in order to pull the vertical threads in to restore the original shape. Thread the chenille needle with a single strand of the second colour and attach this with a double stitch to the tassel head at the concave part nearest the neck (see Fig 7.14). Wrap the thread as evenly as possible round the concave section of the shape, forming a band of horizontal colour and pulling in the vertical

Fig 7.14
Attaching the horizontal binding thread.

Fig 7.13  The vertical wrapping complete.

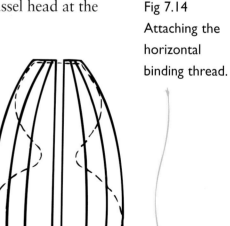

Fig 7.15  Wrapping a concave section horizontally to pull in the vertical threads.

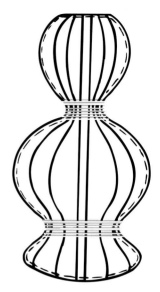

Fig 7.16  The direction of the binding – vertical and horizontal – to reveal the shape of the head.

threads (see Figs 7.15 and 7.16). Secure the thread by working it into the threads beneath the horizontal wrapping. Repeat the process wherever you wish to reveal the concave shapes of the head.

7 Attach the hanging loop on the wire, secure and cut off any excess (see pages 74–5).

8 Complete the tassel by making the skirt from all the thread left over after making the hanging cord and winding the head. Attach it to the head in the normal way (see pages 72–3).

9 Tie the decorative cord round the top of the skirt to neaten the join (see Fig 7.17). The cord can be enhanced with beads for extra interest.

Fig 7.17  The completed tassel.

✒ PROJECT ✒

# TASSEL DECORATED WITH MINI-TASSELS

Adding mini-tassels to a skirt is akin to using beads as decorations, as explained in Chapter 5, pages 56–8. It provides an opportunity to add colour and texture, and to use different threads from those contained in the main skirt. Mini-tassels are easy and fun to make (they are simply small, one-part thread tassels): it is even possible to make a complete skirt from them.

## Materials and equipment

- Completed two-part tassel ready for decoration
- Card for individual tassel templates

*or*

- Purpose-made thread winder (which allows you to wind a number of tassels simultaneously, see Fig 7.18)

*or*

- Piece of wood or hardboard 8 x 30cm (3⅛ x 11¾in) (this is what I use and it is just as good as a proper thread-winder – a winding board of this size will make six 5cm (2in) mini-tassels in one go)
- Masking tape or other lightly adhesive tape (see page 15)
- 2 reels of Burmilana thread, each of a different colour (this is for the mini-tassels and cords – 1 reel will be enough if you are using only one colour)
- Cotton Perle or Cebelia thread for temporary ties
- Chenille needle size 20
- Pencil and dark-coloured felt-tip pen

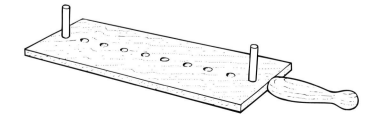

Fig 7.18 A purpose-made thread winder.

# Method

1 Make the number of cords you require – 12 are needed for this project to hang the mini-tassels. Each cord should be made from 1m (1yd) of the Burmilana thread.

2 Next make a heavy cord to neaten the neck after the mini-tassels have been attached. I used six 2m (2yd 6in) lengths of the Burmilana (three of each colour) folded in half.

3 Make the preparations for winding the mini-tassels (12 are needed for this project), which have an overall length of 5cm (2in). There are three options, depending on whether you are using card templates, a thread winder or a piece of wood:

(a) Cut and prepare the template card(s) in the correct proportions (see page 34). You can make an individual card for each tassel, or make just one card and use it repeatedly.

(b) Set up the thread winder with as great a distance in centimetres, divisible by 10 (or in inches, divisible by 4), as you can get.

(c) Mark the piece of wood with a pencil line at 5cm (2in) intervals, as shown in Fig 7.19. Then take the felt-tip pen and mark the first 5cm (2in) line again, then mark every alternate one in the same way. You will need to mark both sides of the wood as for the card templates used earlier (see page 34). Cover the wood with a piece of clingfilm to prevent snagging threads.

**TIP** I often work out how much thread I am using up by first weighing the reels before starting to wind the tassels. Burmilana reels hold 25g of thread, but weigh 28g with the reel included. Note the starting weight, then weigh the reel again when you have used enough thread to make a tassel. Keep a record of these weights as a reference for the next time you wish to use that particular type of thread.

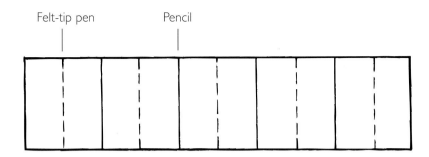

Felt-tip pen          Pencil

Fig 7.19 The markings necessary for a wooden winding board.

4 (a) If you are using individual cards, wind all the mini-tassels and apply tying threads at the neck and skirt bottom (see Chapter 4). Use the cords made in step 1 to tie the tops, as for hanging cords on basic thread tassels (see page 36).

(b) If you are using a thread winder, tie the thread on and wind it round the posts. After winding, tie the thread with cord at intervals. The first tie should be 5cm (2in) from one end, the second should be 10cm (4in) away from the first. Continue tying at 10cm (4in) intervals, ending with 5cm (2in) at the other end. If there is thread to spare, because the winder is longer than you need, mark the beginning of the unwanted thread with a different colour. The gap between each tie is twice as long as the finished tassels will be. The cords are tied at what will be the top of each tassel, so to remove the tassels correctly from the winder you must cut the threads at the exact halfway point between each tie. Fold each cut tassel over and tie the neck firmly with fine Cotton Perle or Cebelia thread.

(c) If you are using a marked piece of wood, anchor the thread at one end with masking tape and wind the thread on lengthways. Anchor the final end of thread with masking tape also. Tie the tassels with cords at the intervals marked in felt-tip pen (these will be the tops of the tassels) (see Fig 7.20). Remember to tie cords round the thread on both sides of the board. Now place a piece of masking tape across the threads between each mark on the board. This will hold the threads steady during cutting and stop them springing out of line. Cut the tassels halfway between each tie, at the points marked in pencil only. Fold each tassel in half and tie the neck firmly with Cotton Perle or Cebelia.

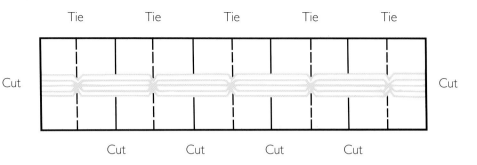

Fig 7.20  Thread
and ties in place
on the winding
board.

5 Trim the mini-tassels and, if necessary, dip in water, straighten and trim again. If you are using Burmilana thread it will not need to be dipped in water to straighten.

6 Each mini-tassel now needs to have its neck bound with decorative cord or thread. Thread the cord on to the chenille needle and bury the knotted end in the tassel head, bringing the needle out at the neck. Wrap the neck, covering the tying thread as you wind (or you can remove it once the neck is sufficiently secure). Finish off firmly. Complete each mini-tassel in this way.

7 The mini-tassels are now ready to fasten to the skirt of the main tassel. They can be stitched individually by their hanging cords on to the neck of the main tassel, or you can use the method described for attaching threaded beads on pages 57–8. The tassels are best hung at even spaces round the skirt, but they do not have to be all the same length. Try out different effects by pulling up the

**TIP**  Use the board (or any other flat surface) to help you tie the necks of the mini-tassels. Place the tassel sideways on to the board and tape across it. Pull the cord at the top gently away from the tassel, until the threads are straight and taut, and tape this down also (see Fig 7.21). Put the tying thread under the tassel where you wish to tie the neck. Remember that damping the thread helps to hold the knot tightly, so have a saucer of water to hand. Tie the neck tightly and release the tassel. The tape can be re-used.

Fig 7.21  A mini-tassel taped to the board to aid neck tying.

Fig 7.22  The finished tassel with mini-tassel skirt decoration.

hanging cords to make some of the mini-tassels hang higher. Any excess hanging cord can be cut off once the tassels are secured in place.

8 Now neaten the neck by binding on the heavy cord made in step 2 – or use a decorative thread such as Sundance – to hide the ends of the mini-tassel hanging cords. Tie the cord on with a knot, or stitch it neatly round the top of the skirt, cutting off any surplus cord (see Fig 7.22).

## ❦ PROJECT ❦
# DECORATED BOUND HEADS

Fig 7.23 overleaf shows a selection of tassels with decorated bound heads, to show some of the varied effects which can be achieved. The Method simply sets out ways of attaching different decorative items to the tassel head. It is basically just common sense.

Fig 7.23 A selection of tassels with decorated bound heads: just a few of the many possibilities.

# Materials and equipment

- Completed two-part tassel with bound head and skirt
- Beading needle size 10
- Crewel needle size 10
- A selection of decorative items – beads, sequins, covered buttons, needlelace flowers, ribbon or braid flowers and decorative threads can all be used
- Rayon 40 or Sylko 40 in a colour to match the tassel head and skirt

# Method

1 Beads and sequins are fixed to the head by stitching into the threads or cords covering the wooden shape. You cannot, of course, stitch right through a solid head, but the binding thread will provide a sufficient anchor for such lightweight items.

2 Small buttons can be fixed on in the same manner as beads and sequins. Antique shops sometimes have cards of attractive and unusual old buttons. If you are prepared to do some fiddly work, then small self-coverable buttons can be made with material which complements the colours of the tassel.

3 Braid flowers can be made by cutting 5cm (2in) lengths of braid, Offray ribbon or silk ribbon. With a matching thread in the crewel needle (size 10) work a double stitch at one end of the braid or ribbon and then work small running stitches along to the other end. Pull the thread up tight so that the braid curls round. Attach the two ends by working another double stitch into the end where you started, and secure the thread. If you are ready to attach the flower to the tassel head, do so now without cutting off the thread. Slip stitch is the best means of fixing the flower securely to the head. If you are not ready to attach the flower, cut off the thread, make all the flowers you need and then attach them later.

## ❧ PROJECT ❧

# MIXED-THREAD HEAD AND SKIRT WITH DECORATED NECK

By now you should be able to choose threads, make cords, wind tassels and cover shaped heads with some confidence. Here is a chance to bring all the skills you have learnt so far into play for one tassel. The details of materials given below are those used to make the tassel shown, but you should branch out and pick your own colours and textures to create something unique.

The instructions which follow give an alternative method for making a skirt. You can use the normal method if you prefer: just remember to apply the method for wrapping the colours given here.

## Materials and equipment

- Shaped wooden head
- 1 reel Decor thread
- One 25g (1oz) ball of Lamé (holds 150m (164yd) of thread) or 1 ball of Nora thread
- 1 reel of Burmilana thread
- Cebelia thread (for overlapping backstitch)
- Card for skirt template
- PVA glue and small brush
- Chenille needle size 20

## Method

1 Make cords from your three chosen colours and threads (making the cords from single colours only) and cover the wooden shape with these cords (see pages 69–71), alternating the colours as you work down the head. Cover the neck with cord so that you can stitch into it when attaching the skirt. The hanging cord can be added at this stage also.

Fig 7.24 Card template marked up for the alternative method for skirt making.

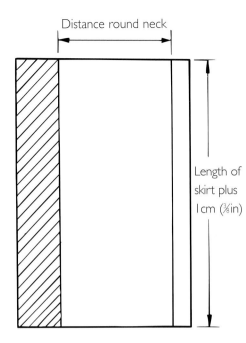

Distance round neck

Length of skirt plus 1cm (⅜in)

Start by anchoring the sewing thread with a double stitch

Secure top of skirt with overlapping backstitch

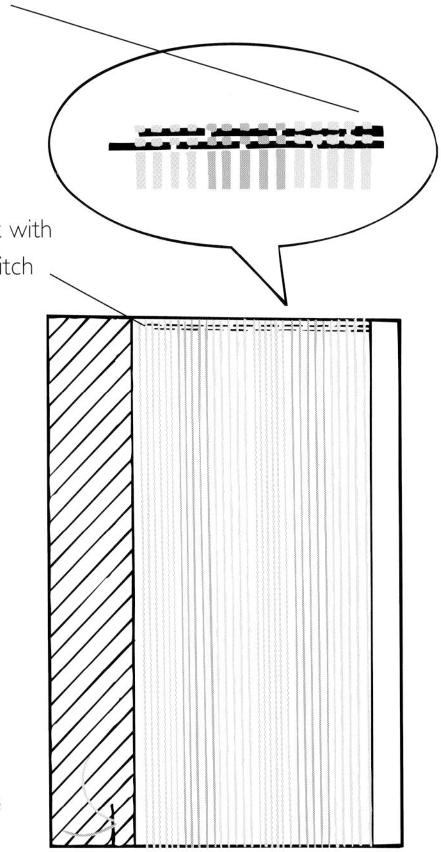

Fig 7.25 Overlapping backstitch at the top of the card.

2 Cut a piece of card the length you require the skirt to be, plus 1cm (⅜in), and as wide as the distance round the neck, plus 10cm (4in). Mark the neck measurement on the card as shown in Fig 7.24, leaving 7cm (2¾in) to hold on the left and 3cm (1¼in) spare on the right. (If you are left-handed, reverse these instructions.)

3 Take one colour of thread, anchor it in a slit in the card, and begin to wind it round the card, between the neck measurements you marked on the template, starting from the left (or the right if you are left-handed). Keep winding until you have covered one-sixth of the card. Anchor the thread in a slit at the bottom of the card and cut it off just below the level of the card. Anchor the next colour and work across another one-sixth of the card in the same way. Work the third colour, then repeat the whole process with the three colours once again. You will now have covered the whole of the area marked on the card for the neck (see Fig 7.25).

4 Thread the chenille needle with Cebelia thread and

anchor this with a double stitch at the top of the card on the right (or left if you are left-handed) (see Fig 7.25). Use overlapping backstitch to work across the very top of the card, picking up all the skirt threads (make sure you do not miss any). Finish at the other side with a double stitch and remove the skirt from the card by bending the card slightly and easing the threads off.

5 Attach the skirt to the neck with strong thread by slip stitching through the row of overlapping backstitch and into the threads round the bound neck. Take care not to stretch the skirt threads: ease them round the neck and pin in place before beginning to stitch. At the point where the two ends of the skirt meet they must not overlap, as the colour sequence will then be spoiled.

6 There are several different ways of finishing off the neck:

(a) Tie or stitch a heavy cord or decorative thread round the neck.

(b) Make a thick frill (see pages 43–6), attach it securely then cut all the loops to create a fringed effect.

(c) Bead the neck as explained on pages 51–4.

7 Cut and trim the skirt, dampening and straightening if necessary.

My finished tassel is shown in Fig 7.26.

Fig 7.26 The finished tassel with mixed-thread head and skirt, and varied neck decoration.

# Other decorative possibilities

Fig 7.27 shows a tassel with a covered head and frill made from one reel of Jabara, a Madeira braid, with a skirt of Sticku.

The neck frill is made by winding the Jabara round a 2cm (¾in) card template without a slot. As there is no slot, the stitching can only be done on one side of the card (you could either stitch across the very top, or across the middle on one side). Complete the stitching, secure the thread and gently pull the template card out. The frill can then be slip stitched to the neck or attached with wire in a way similar to that described in the next chapter, on page 105.

Fig 7.27
Braided tassel
head and frill.

# CHAPTER 8

# THE POLISHED-HEAD TASSEL

A tassel with a polished wooden head not only looks elegant, but it feels good as well. The smoothness of the polished wood adds something extra to the tassel's tactile properties, contrasting well with the softness of the skirt threads. The choice of wood also contributes to the beauty of the tassel: light or dark woods can be chosen to match up with furnishings; shapes can be varied by the woodturner and left unmuffled by binding cords. If you have no friendly woodturner nearby, the list of suppliers on page 114 will tell you where you might send for a design list.

Polished-head tassels are also easy to make, because all you need to add is a skirt and perhaps a decorative neck cord. There are two types of polished head. One is like the shaped wooden heads used in the previous two chapters, where the skirt is attached to a groove in the neck; the other has no groove, but the central hole is enlarged at the bottom and the skirt is fastened into this. The second type is suitable for making light pulls and for other tassels which will be handled frequently. A project for each type of polished head is given in this chapter. The third project is for making a complete tassel from beads: larger beads make up the head as an alternative to a complete polished head (although you could use a small polished head instead), while loops of smaller beads make up the skirt, offering a different look and feel to the more usual thread skirts.

**TIP**  Polished heads can also be painted if you have the patience and some artistic skill. Why not have a go at seasonal themes for Christmas or Easter decorations; nursery rhyme characters for a child's room; plain colours to match the particular colour scheme of a room. However you choose to paint your tassel head, the method for making the tassel is the same as that described in the projects which follow.

## ❧ PROJECT ❧

# BASIC POLISHED-HEAD TASSEL

## Materials and equipment

- Polished wooden head, with neck groove
- Threads for the skirt (Sticku, Rayon 40, Cotton Perle 3, Decor and Renaissance wool are illustrated in Fig 8.1 as ideas, but pick your own to suit your tastes)
- Hanging cord
- Decorative neck cord (optional)
- Card for skirt template
- Florist's wire or single-strand copper wire
- Small pliers

## Method

Fig 8.1  A selection of threads for use with polished heads.

1 Measure the neck of the polished head and cut a piece of wire twice the neck length.

2 Cut the card template to size and mark up, depending on which method you are using to make the skirt (see pages 71–3 and 98–9).

**TIP** Two methods for making a skirt are included in this book (see pages 71–3 and 98–9). Either method is satisfactory, but I personally prefer the first method outlined in Chapter 6. Although this method requires a large piece of card and is harder to wind if the skirt is long, it is easier to attach neatly to the head.

3 Wind the threads for the skirt on to the card.

4 Stitch through the centre slot in the card (or across the top of the template if you are using the alternative method) and remove the skirt.

5 (a) If you have followed the normal method of stitching the skirt (pages 71–3), place the length of wire over the stitching (see Fig 8.2), then fold the skirt over and pick it up so that it hangs down on both sides of the wire.

(b) If you have followed the alternative method of stitching the skirt (pages 98–9), thread the wire through the loops of the skirt so that the skirt hangs on the wire (see Fig 8.3).

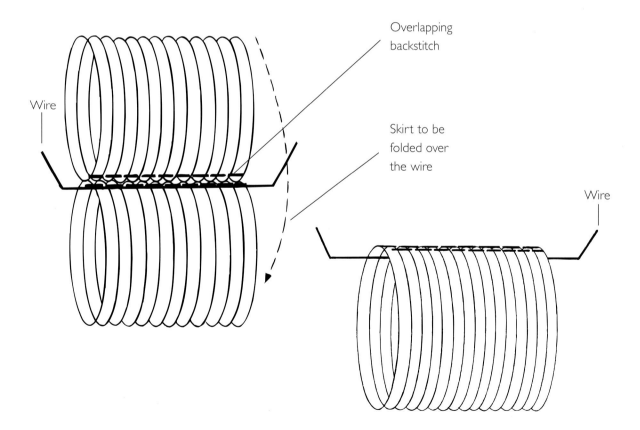

Fig 8.2 Folding the stitched skirt over the wire.

Fig 8.3 Threading the stitched skirt (alternative method) on to the wire.

6 Place the wired skirt round the neck of the polished head, settling it into the groove. Use the pliers to twist the ends of the wire together so that the wire is holding the skirt in place as firmly as possible (see Fig 8.4).

7 Trim the excess twisted wire down to 1cm (⅜in) and tuck this into the neck so that it is hidden in the threads.

8 Add a decorative cord round the neck if you wish.

9 Cut, trim and straighten the tassel, trimming again when it is dry if necessary (see Fig 8.5).

Fig 8.4  The skirt attached to the head with wire.

Fig 8.5  The finished tassel.

## ❧ PROJECT ❧

# LIGHT PULL WITH POLISHED HEAD

## Materials and equipment

- Polished head suitable for use as a light pull (with the central hole enlarged at the bottom, see Fig 8.6)
- Thread for skirt (e.g. Metallic 15, Glamour, Cotton Perle 3 or Sticku would be suitable)
- Card for skirt template
- Hanging cord (either one you have made, or purchased cord may be preferable for a light pull as it will be easier to fix into the switch)
- Small pliers
- PVA adhesive
- Florist's wire or single-strand copper wire
- Sewing thread
- Masking tape

## Method

1 Make up a basic one-part thread tassel (see Chapter 4), but leave the neck tie off. The tying thread at the top should be cut off very close to the knot. This thread remains on the tassel, but will be hidden in the polished head.

2 Put the light pull cord through the centre of the tassel alongside the top tying thread. Pull about 2cm (¾in) of the cord through and tape the two parts of the cord together (see Fig 8.7).

Fig 8.6 A basic thread tassel ready to put together with the polished head.

Fig 8.7 Putting the hanging cord through the tassel and taping it to the main cord.

Tape together, then either wrap with wire or stitch over the tape

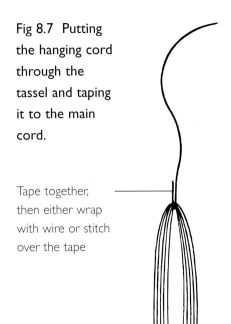

Fig 8.8 The two parts of the cord secured together.

Fig 8.9 Joining the cords to make a hanging loop.

Hanging loop ——————

Joins hidden inside polished head

3 The tape is a temporary measure to hold the cords together. Now you need to secure the join by stitching through the cord or binding with a length of fine wire (see Fig 8.8). A join of this kind should slip easily into the central hole of the polished head, whereas a knotted cord could prevent the thread skirt from fitting properly into the head.

4 If you wish to have a looped hanging cord, secure one end of the cord through the centre of the tassel as described in steps 2 and 3. Secure the other end in a similar fashion as close as possible to the first join (see Fig 8.9), leaving a loop at the top of the size you desire. The wiring or stitching should be as tight as possible in order to lessen the bulk of the cord and to enable both joins to be hidden within the polished head.

Fig 8.10 Pulling the cord through the polished head.

**TIP** Work carefully when applying glue into the hole: if any gets on the outside of the tassel head, wipe it off immediately with a damp cloth. Using a glue container with a nozzle head will reduce the likelihood of unwanted mess.

5 Now thread the long cord or loop up through the wooden tassel head. Pull it through so that the tassel on the end of the cord is just about to enter the head (see Fig 8.10). At this point, half-fill the hole at the bottom of the head with PVA glue. Be quite generous with the glue as it needs to penetrate the threads.

6 Pull the cord further through the head so that the top of the tassel goes right into the hole (see Fig 8.9). Pull the cord as firmly as possible to wedge the tassel securely into the hole and on to the glue. The joins in the cord should be hidden inside the head.

7 Turn the head upside down and add more glue into the threads inside the head.

8 Allow the glue to dry thoroughly before cutting the skirt, trimming and straightening (see Fig 8.11).

Fig 8.11 The finished light pull tassel.

# TASSEL MADE FROM BEADS

All sorts of beads can be used to make complete tassels: the possible combinations are endless. It is also a wonderful way of using up old beads. This project uses several large beads to make an alternative polished head, but you could use an ordinary polished head instead and still attach the bead skirt as described below.

The beads for the head must be larger than those used for the skirt. For the tassel shown here I used four beads of graded sizes for the head.

For the skirt I used seed beads, which can be bought loose or ready strung on fine cord. If you wish to make a beaded tassel very quickly, then the ready strung beads will be ideal. If these are not to hand, you will need to thread the beads on to fine thread or cord so that you have a long length ready for use (see Method). The tassel in this project is 8cm (3⅛in) long, and involves 1,000 seed beads in all. The beads are strung on a single strand of Rainbow thread, and the hanging cord is made from the Rainbow also.

## Materials and equipment

- 2 large beads, or up to 4 beads of graded sizes, for the tassel head
- A selection of smaller beads for the skirt (approx. 1,000 needed)
- Beading needle size 10 (or a fine sewing needle if it fits through the beads)
- A card of Rainbow thread, or fine nylon thread – the kind used for invisible hemming (if you decide to make a cord rather than use the thread plain, make sure it will go through the beads and the needle eye)

> **TIP**  If you are making cord on which to thread the beads, you need to make a sufficient length to make all the loops for the skirt, the hanging cord and about 20cm (8in) for finishing off (see Method).

# Method

**1** First make an experimental loop of beads twice the length of the tassel you are going to make. The tassel in this project is 8cm (3⅛in) long, so the loop will be 16cm (6¼in) long (see Fig 8.12). Count the number of beads you have used for this one loop (a loop made with my beads used 100) and make a note of the amount. To calculate the total number of beads you need, simply multiply the amount of beads for one loop by the number of loops you think you need: in this case 10 loops were used, giving a total of 1,000 beads.

Fig 8.12 A loop of beads.

**2** Now make the hanging cord from six or eight lengths of Rainbow, to whatever size you need.

**3** Thread the beading needle with 1m (1yd) of thread and tie a knot at the end.

**4** Thread the beads for one loop on to the thread, then work a backstitch into the last bead (see Fig 8.13). Now thread the needle through the first bead of this first loop and then continue by

Fig 8.13 The method for securing the beads in their loops.

**TIP** If you are using cord instead of plain thread and have trouble threading it on to the beading needle, you could use 10cm (4in) of fine fuse wire instead. Put the wire through the looped end of the cord, bend the wire in half and twist the two pieces together to act as the needle.

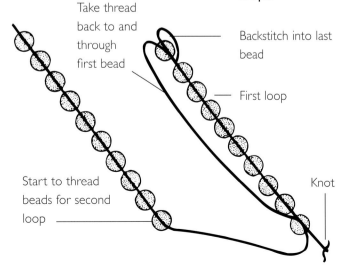

Take thread back to and through first bead

Backstitch into last bead

First loop

Start to thread beads for second loop

Knot

Fig 8.14  All the loops finished and joined together.

Fig 8.15  Threading the hanging cord through the beads for the head.

Fig 8.16  The hanging cord threaded through head beads and skirt loops.

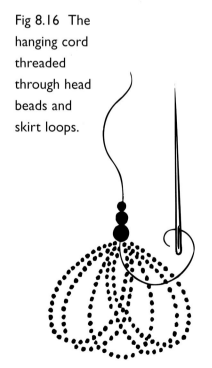

threading on the beads for the second loop. Work a backstitch through the last bead on the second loop and then thread the needle through the first bead of that loop. Continue in this way until you have made all the loops (see Fig 8.14).

5 When all the beads are on the cord, secure the thread by taking the needle halfway down through the beads on one of the loops and then working a backstitch through one bead. Continue threading the needle down to the bottom of that loop and cut off the thread.

6 Now take the hanging cord you have made and thread it from top to bottom through the larger beads you have chosen for the tassel head (see Fig 8.15) (or the complete polished

head if you are using one instead). Then thread it through the tops of the bead loops of the skirt, and back up through the head beads (see Fig 8.16). Tie the two ends of the cord together (with the knot at the top) to form a hanging loop and to prevent the top beads from coming off. Cut off the cord. The completed tassel is shown in Fig 8.17, along with a bead tassel made with a light pull head.

Fig 8.17
Finished bead
tassels.

# LIST OF SUPPLIERS

**Barnyarns Ltd**
PO Box 28
Thirsk
N Yorkshire
YO7 3YN
Tel: 01845 524344

**The Bead Warehouse**
43 Neal Street
Covent Garden
London
WC2H 9PJ
Tel: 0171 240 0931

**Craft Basics**
9 Gillygate
York
YO3 7EA
Tel: 01904 52840

**Dainty Supplies Ltd**
35 Phoenix Road
Crowther Industrial
  Estate
Washington 3
Tyne and Wear
Tel: 0191 416 7886

**French Knots**
12 Gwydr Crescent
Uplands
Swansea
W Glamorgan
SA2 0AA
Tel: 01792 653279

**Hanneke's Handicrafts**
Mansk-Svenska Pub. Co.
17 North View
Peel, Isle of Man
IM5 1DQ
Tel: 01624 844241

**Inca Studio**
10 Duke Street
Princes Risborough
Bucks
HP27 0AT
Tel: 01844 343343

**John Lewis Partnership
Stores**
(check a telephone
directory for your local
branch)

**MKC Ltd**
92 Kirkgate
Leeds
West Yorkshire
LS2 7DJ
Tel: 0113 245 3156

**Northgate Needlecraft**
160 Northgate Street
Great Yarmouth
Norfolk
NR30 1BY
Tel: 01493 843604

**Red Cottage Crafts**
1 Rawdon Court
Main Street
Moira
Co Down
BT67 0LQ
Tel: 01846 619172

**Stitches**
7 The Terrace
Market Dew Street
Penzance
Cornwall
Tel: 01736 50312

**Teazle Embroideries**
35 Boothferry Road
Hull
N Humberside
HU3 6AU
Tel: 01482 572531

**Tenterden Rushcraft**
The Craft Centre
Station Road
Tenterden
Kent
TN30 6JB
Tel: 015806 3326

**Terry Taylor**
(for polished heads)
Yew Tree House
35 Station Road
Snainton
Scarborough
YO13 9AP
Tel: 01723 859500

**Voirrey Embroidery**
Brimstage Hall
Brimstage
Wirral
L63 6JA
Tel: 0151 342 3514

*NB: All Madeira thread
stockists should also stock
unpolished tassel heads.
Order polished heads from a
local woodturner if possible.*

# FURTHER READING

Bullen, Jenny, *The Madeira Book of Embroidery Stitches*, A & C Black, 1990 (paperback, Madeira Threads (UK) Ltd, 1990)

Crutchley, Anna, *The Tassels Book*, Lorenz Books, 1996

Dickens, Susan, *The Art of Tassel Making*, Allen & Unwin, 1984

Welch, Nancy, *Tassels: The Fanciful Embellishment*, Lark Books, 1992

# ABOUT THE AUTHOR

Enid Taylor was born and educated in Skipton, Yorkshire. After training as a Home Economics teacher in London, she taught in schools, colleges and teacher training college for 24 years.

In 1982 she left the teaching profession to start her own business. Her first venture was a Craft Studio where she taught lacemaking, spinning and needlework, and visiting teachers gave weekend courses. The Studio also provided an outlet for a wide range of British handicrafts as well as being a popular tea-room. As a second venture she set up a successful embroidery and craft shop in Scarborough.

Enid has arranged several lace and embroidery exhibitions at Scarborough Art Gallery. She is also involved in the organization

of the annual Craft, Embroidery and Fashion Exhibition run by Madeira Threads (UK) in Harrogate.

Enid and her husband Terry now live in the countryside near Scarborough. She does some teaching and consultancy work, and finds time for needlework, in between gardening and helping her son who runs a local hotel.

# INDEX